The 8-Week Plan to Get a New Job:

Build Confidence, Master Interviews, and Find Work That Inspires You

PUBLISHED BY Arcana Horizons Editions

© Copyright 2025 - All rights reserved.

All introductions, analyses, and commentaries contained within this book may not be reproduced, duplicated, or transmitted without direct written permission from the author or the publisher. Under no circumstances will any blame or legal responsibility be held against the publisher or author for any damages, reparation, or monetary loss due to the information contained within this book, either directly or indirectly.

Legal Notice:

This book is only for personal use. You cannot amend, distribute, sell, use, quote, or paraphrase any part of the introductions, analyses, or commentaries within this book, without the consent of the author or publisher.

Disclaimer Notice:

Please note the information contained within this document is for educational and entertainment purposes only. All efforts have been executed to present accurate, up-to-date, reliable, complete information. No warranties of any kind are declared or implied. Readers acknowledge that the author is not engaged in the rendering of legal, financial, medical, or professional advice. The content within this book has been derived from various sources. Please consult a licensed professional before attempting any techniques outlined in this book.

By reading this document, the reader agrees that under no circumstances is the author responsible for any losses, direct or indirect, that are incurred as a result of the use of the information contained within this document, including, but not limited to, errors, omissions, or inaccuracies.

Table of contents

Introduction 4

Chapter 1: Clarity Before Action — Defining Your Direction.. 9

Chapter 2: Building a Personal Narrative That Stands Out.. 21

Chapter 3: Crafting an Application That Opens Doors 33

Chapter 4: Mastering the Art of Networking..... 45

Chapter 5: Preparing for the Interview with Confidence and Clarity.. 58

Chapter 6: Navigating the Interview with Presence and Poise... 72

Chapter 7: Answering Questions with Strategy and Substance 85

Chapter 8: Asking Questions That Build Connection and Insight.. 99

Chapter 9: Navigating Offers and Negotiations with Confidence 112

Conclusion: Stepping Into the Next Chapter with Confidence 126

Introduction

Finding a new job isn't just about sending out résumés or rehearsing answers to predictable interview questions. It's about rediscovering who you are, what you want, and how you want to show up in the world every morning when you wake up. If you're holding this book, chances are you're standing at a crossroads. Maybe you're tired of a job that drains you. Maybe you're returning to the workforce after a break. Maybe you're ready to stretch beyond what's familiar and chase something more meaningful. Whatever brought you here, this is the moment you begin to shape a future that actually excites you.

The next eight weeks aren't just about finding a job. They're about building the inner and outer toolkit you need to claim work that reflects your strengths, your values, and your aspirations.

For most people, job searching comes with a storm of emotions: hope, fear, impatience, excitement, frustration, and doubt. It's a vulnerable process. You put your story out into the world and hope someone recognizes your value. But here's the truth most people never say out loud: a successful job search doesn't start with getting others to say yes to you. It starts with *you* saying yes to yourself.

That's why this book doesn't jump straight into cover letters and interview questions. Instead, it begins by grounding you in clarity, confidence, and strategy. The eight-week structure is designed intentionally. It's a clear, steady path that transforms what often feels like chaos into something you can actually manage. Instead of waking up each day overwhelmed by a flood of job listings, you'll follow a structured plan. Each week builds upon the last, guiding you step by step toward your goal—not just *any* job, but the *right* one.

The 8-Week Plan to Get a New Job

This process has been shaped by real career journeys—people who transitioned from uncertainty to clarity, from fear to confidence, from scattered searching to strategic action. It works because it addresses both the inner and outer dimensions of a job search. Confidence and strategy. Vision and execution.

Over the next eight weeks, you'll learn how to articulate your strengths with precision, present your story with impact, and enter interviews with the grounded confidence of someone who knows what they bring to the table. You'll learn to treat your job search like a project with a plan, not a random lottery ticket you keep scratching, hoping for luck.

But before we get practical, let's address the emotional reality. Job searching can be lonely. The waiting, the silence after applications, the rejections that arrive in your inbox at 9:00 p.m. when you least expect them. It can feel personal, even when it isn't. It can chip away at your self-esteem if you let it. That's why this plan doesn't treat confidence like a motivational slogan. It treats it like a muscle—one you'll train, week after week, so it grows stronger even when the results haven't arrived yet.

You'll begin by clarifying your direction. Because a vague job search leads to vague results. When you know exactly what kind of work energizes you, what industries align with your skills, and what environments bring out your best, your search becomes more focused and far more effective.

You'll then build your personal narrative—the story that connects your past to the future you want to create. Employers don't hire bullet points on a résumé; they hire people with stories that make sense. When you can express who you are, why your experience matters, and what makes you different, your applications stop sounding like everyone else's.

Then we'll get tactical. We'll craft résumés and LinkedIn profiles that actually *work*—that cut through automated systems and get human eyes on your application. We'll map out your networking strategy so opportunities start finding you, instead of the other way around. You'll learn to reach out without feeling like you're begging for a favor. You'll learn to present yourself with confidence rather than apology.

And when interviews come, you won't walk in hoping for the best. You'll walk in prepared. That means more than rehearsing answers—it means learning how to connect with your interviewer as a human being, how to show your value without sounding rehearsed, and how to stay calm when the unexpected happens. You'll learn how to navigate behavioral questions, tricky scenarios, salary negotiations, and the subtle ways people evaluate whether you're the right fit.

But perhaps most importantly, you'll learn how to hold onto yourself throughout the process. A job search shouldn't be about shrinking yourself to fit a box. It should be about finding the right shape for your talents, your personality, and your ambitions.

This plan is divided into eight focused weeks:

- **Week 1** is about clarity—defining what you want, what you offer, and why it matters.
- **Week 2** focuses on building your personal narrative and professional branding.
- **Week 3** is dedicated to creating powerful application materials that stand out.
- **Week 4** helps you master networking strategically and authentically.
- **Week 5** prepares you for every stage of the interview process.
- **Week 6** focuses on negotiation and confidently claiming your worth.

- **Week 7** strengthens your mindset and resilience, turning uncertainty into momentum.
- **Week 8** is about execution—putting everything together to land the offer that aligns with your goals.

Each week combines reflection, action steps, and practical tools. You won't just read; you'll *do*. This isn't another book that leaves you with vague inspiration. It's a structured roadmap designed to produce tangible results.

Throughout the process, I'll also share proven strategies drawn from recruiters, hiring managers, and career coaches who have helped thousands of candidates land positions across industries. You'll see how small shifts in your approach—like how you phrase an accomplishment or how you follow up after an interview—can create outsized results.

Equally important, we'll dismantle the myths that hold people back. The myth that you need to be "the perfect candidate" to be hired. The myth that networking is only for extroverts. The myth that rejection means you're not good enough. Once you start seeing these myths for what they are—false stories that have no power unless you give it to them—you'll navigate the search with a lighter, stronger step.

There's something transformative about taking control of your job search. The moment you shift from "waiting to be chosen" to "choosing where you want to go," everything changes. That doesn't mean the path will be effortless. It means it will be yours.

Some weeks will feel energizing. Others may challenge you. There will be moments of doubt, and that's okay. That's part of the process. Growth rarely happens in perfect straight lines. But with a clear structure beneath your feet, doubt doesn't have to derail you.

By the end of these eight weeks, the way you approach work—and yourself—will be different. You'll no longer define your worth by a line in a job description. You'll recognize the power you already hold. You'll know how to articulate it, how to negotiate for it, and how to step into a new chapter with clarity instead of fear.

This isn't a fantasy. It's a process. And you're about to begin it.

You don't have to have it all figured out today. All you need is the willingness to take the first step. One focused week at a time, we'll build the momentum that gets you from uncertainty to opportunity, from frustration to fulfillment, from where you are now to where you want to be.

A new job can change your schedule. The right job can change your life. Let's make sure the next one does exactly that.

Chapter 1: Clarity Before Action — Defining Your Direction

1.1 Reclaiming Your Sense of Purpose

Before you can land the job you want, you have to understand what you actually want—and why. This might sound obvious at first, but it's the step most people rush through or skip altogether. They fire off résumés to anything that seems remotely close to their skills. They scroll through job boards late at night, clicking "apply" almost on autopilot. They say yes to interviews that don't excite them and accept offers that feel "good enough" but not aligned with their deeper goals.

Clarity isn't a luxury. It's the foundation of an effective job search. Without it, everything else becomes guesswork: your applications are scattered, your networking lacks focus, and your interviews feel like you're trying to convince yourself just as much as the employer. But when your goals are clear, your actions become intentional. You don't just look for work—you seek opportunities that actually match your values, strengths, and ambitions.

Reclaiming your sense of purpose begins with slowing down before you speed up. It means stepping out of the frantic rhythm of job listings and stepping into an honest conversation with yourself. Who are you becoming? What kind of work energizes you, not just in theory but in lived experience? What kind of problems do you feel drawn to solve? When you strip away titles and salaries for a moment, what kind of contribution actually feels meaningful to you?

Many people are uncomfortable asking themselves these questions because they reveal how much we've been trained to think about work in transactional terms: find a job, earn a paycheck, repeat. But the job market has shifted. Employers don't just want skill sets—they want people who are clear, confident, and aligned with their own missions. And more importantly, *you* deserve more than just a paycheck. You deserve work that doesn't make you dread Mondays, work that engages your mind, respects your time, and gives your days a sense of direction.

The search for purpose isn't some abstract spiritual exercise. It's practical. Clarity gives you sharper language to describe your value to others. It helps you filter out opportunities that will waste your time. It strengthens your confidence in interviews because you're not trying to become what someone else wants—you're standing in what you already know to be true about yourself.

Start by reflecting on your work history—not just the roles you've had, but how each one made you feel. Which projects made the hours fly by? Which responsibilities gave you a sense of accomplishment long after you'd left the office? Which situations drained you no matter how well you performed? Purpose often hides in the details we overlook: the kind of conversations that light us up, the type of impact we want to make, the environments where we naturally thrive.

Think about moments when you felt fully engaged—not because someone praised you, but because the work itself mattered to you. Maybe it was solving a tough problem, mentoring someone, designing a better system, creating something from scratch, or leading a team through a challenge. These aren't random memories. They are signposts pointing toward your personal zone of meaning.

Once you've identified these signposts, go deeper. Ask yourself why they matter. If you loved mentoring someone, was it because you enjoy seeing others grow? If you thrived on solving complex problems, is it because clarity out of chaos energizes you? If you loved working on a collaborative project, was it because you crave a sense of shared mission? Understanding the *why* behind what drives you will help you look beyond surface-level job titles and target roles that actually align with what fulfills you.

A practical way to do this is through what I call a "purpose map." Take a blank sheet of paper. In the center, write down a single word: **Impact**. Then draw branches outward in different directions. On each branch, write down something that gives your work meaning. It might be "teaching," "creating," "helping," "building," "organizing," "leading," or "innovating." Once you have your branches, add specific examples underneath each. These examples should come from your own lived experiences—times when you felt most alive, engaged, or proud of your contribution.

When you step back and look at your purpose map, patterns begin to emerge. You might see that the moments that made you happiest all involved collaboration, or that they all centered around creative problem-solving. You might realize that, even though your previous job title said "analyst," what really lit you up was coaching junior colleagues. These patterns are far more revealing than job descriptions ever will be.

Reclaiming purpose also means letting go of inherited expectations. So many of us carry silent scripts written by family, culture, or past experiences: what counts as a "good job," what kind of work is "safe," what success is supposed to look like. These scripts shape our choices more than we realize. Maybe you've stayed in a field because it seemed practical, even though it left you drained. Maybe you've avoided pursuing something more meaningful because it didn't fit the image of what people expected from you.

But here's the truth: purpose doesn't need permission. No one else gets to define what meaningful work looks like for you. This first week is your opportunity to step back from external noise and reconnect with your own voice. That doesn't mean ignoring financial realities or responsibilities—it means making them part of a vision rather than the entire vision.

The clarity you're seeking isn't about coming up with a perfect, unchanging life plan. It's about identifying the direction that feels real to you *now*, based on who you are and who you want to become. It's a compass, not a cage. That compass will guide your decisions over the next eight weeks and beyond.

Here's something worth remembering: when you can clearly articulate your purpose, you stop competing for every job. You start attracting the right ones. You start writing applications that feel authentic rather than forced. Your interviews stop being performances and become conversations. And when an offer comes along that doesn't align with your vision, you'll have the clarity and confidence to say no—not from fear, but from strength.

This is why the first week of this plan is dedicated to clarity. Without it, even the best résumé won't get you where you truly want to go. But with it, every other step becomes easier. It informs your branding, sharpens your networking, strengthens your negotiation position, and, perhaps most importantly, helps you recognize a good opportunity when it comes.

Purpose doesn't have to be a grand, world-changing mission. For some, it's building great products. For others, it's supporting a team, solving meaningful problems, or helping people live better lives. What matters is that it's yours.

As you work through this chapter, give yourself permission to be honest—even if that honesty surprises you. If you've outgrown your current path, admit it. If a hidden ambition has been whispering to you for years, let it speak louder. The clarity you find here isn't something you need to justify to anyone else. It's a gift to yourself, and it's the starting line of your next chapter.

Over the coming pages, you'll explore questions and exercises that help you identify your unique drivers. You'll learn to separate what matters to *you* from what's been handed down by others. And when you reach the end of this section, you won't just have vague hopes—you'll have a tangible sense of direction.

This isn't about rushing to define the rest of your life. It's about reclaiming your agency in the present. Because once you know where you want to go, even if the path isn't perfectly clear yet, you can begin to walk with purpose. And that single shift—walking with purpose instead of drifting in uncertainty—can change everything.

1.2 Uncovering Your Core Strengths

Once you've begun to reconnect with your purpose, the next crucial step is understanding the strengths you bring to the table. Many people underestimate how powerful this stage is. They leap into job applications without ever taking the time to identify what truly makes them valuable—not just on paper, but in action. Strength isn't about memorizing a list of skills or echoing buzzwords like "team player" or "problem solver." It's about seeing your unique contribution with clear, steady eyes.

Most of us grow up with a strange relationship to our strengths. We downplay them, assuming they're obvious to everyone. We think, *Well, that's just something I do—it's nothing special.* But the things that come easily to you are often the very things others struggle with. That natural ease is a clue. Your strengths are not just what you're good at—they're what you bring to an organization that others can't replicate in quite the same way.

Start by looking back at the moments in your professional or personal history when you felt genuinely competent. Not just proud of completing a task, but in your element—fully present, capable, and engaged. Maybe you've led a team through a tough deadline, and your calm presence kept everyone moving forward. Maybe you're the person people come to when something complex needs to be made simple. Maybe you're gifted at seeing connections others overlook, or at giving clear direction when things get chaotic.

Strengths reveal themselves not just in achievements but in patterns. Consider the kinds of problems people consistently trust you to solve. Think about the feedback you've received over the years, both formal and informal. Did colleagues often thank you for your patience, your creativity, your organizational skills, your resourcefulness? Did you find yourself stepping into certain roles naturally, not because you were asked to but because it felt right?

It's easy to confuse strengths with credentials. But a strength doesn't always come with a certificate. Someone might have a degree in engineering but their true strength lies in explaining technical concepts to non-technical people. Another might be in marketing but their real value is their ability to build strong, lasting relationships. When you define your strengths clearly, you stop hiding behind titles. You start communicating your value as a person—not just a résumé.

Another powerful way to uncover your strengths is to examine the kinds of challenges that energize you. Most people assume they should avoid difficulties, but the right kind of difficulty can reveal what you're made for. If navigating messy situations excites you rather than drains you, chances are you have a talent for problem-solving. If presenting ideas to a crowd fills you with energy rather than fear, communication may be a strength. If improving inefficient systems gives you a thrill, perhaps your strength lies in strategic thinking or operational excellence.

It's also important to recognize that strengths are not fixed. Some are innate, others are built through years of experience, and some emerge when you're put in the right environment. A strength may have been lying dormant simply because your last role never gave it space to breathe. That's why job transitions are powerful—they give you permission to reexamine not just what you can do, but what you *want* to be known for.

You might be tempted to compare your strengths to someone else's. But comparison is a trap. Your strengths don't need to look impressive on a LinkedIn headline to be real. A quiet ability to resolve conflicts can be just as valuable as flashy technical skills. A talent for noticing details can make or break a project. A calm, stabilizing presence can keep a team afloat when everything else seems uncertain. These qualities might not always make the loudest noise, but they build trust—and trust is currency in any workplace.

Once you've identified your strengths, the real transformation happens when you learn to articulate them with precision. Vague statements like "I'm good with people" or "I'm a hard worker" don't move anyone. But when you can say, "I have a proven ability to build relationships across departments and resolve conflicts before they escalate," or "I excel at creating structure in fast-moving environments," you shift from sounding generic to sounding credible.

And it's not about bragging. It's about owning what's true. Employers want to know what value you bring, and you can't expect them to guess. A well-defined sense of your strengths doesn't just make your applications more persuasive; it changes how you carry yourself. When you know your worth, you stop auditioning for roles that don't deserve your energy. You start choosing the ones that do.

This clarity also empowers you to navigate interviews with more confidence. Instead of grasping for answers when someone asks, "What are your strengths?" you'll have concrete stories ready—stories rooted in real experience. And stories are powerful. They stick in people's minds in ways lists of skills never can.

But uncovering strengths isn't just about talking to employers. It's also about talking to yourself differently. When self-doubt creeps in, as it often does during a job search, knowing your strengths gives you something solid to hold onto. It becomes the ground beneath your feet when external validation is scarce. It allows you to approach the process not as a desperate candidate begging to be chosen, but as a capable professional evaluating opportunities on your own terms.

One of the most liberating realizations in this journey is that your strengths may not fit into neat boxes. You might be someone who bridges technical and creative worlds. You might combine analytical precision with emotional intelligence. That unique blend is your advantage. It's what makes your contribution irreplaceable.

As you continue this week, give yourself permission to look at your strengths with honesty, not modesty. Not everything that matters can be measured in metrics. Some of the most impactful strengths are quiet ones. But when you recognize them, when you name them clearly, you stop moving through the job search as a shadow of yourself. You show up fully—and that changes everything.

1.3 Aligning Your Values with Your Career

Knowing your purpose and strengths is only part of the equation. To build a sustainable, fulfilling career, you need to align those inner elements with the external world of work. This is where values come in—not as vague aspirations, but as guiding principles that shape the kind of professional life you want to build.

Values are often misunderstood. Many people treat them like a decorative poster on a wall—something nice to have, but not essential. In reality, your values are the compass that keeps you from getting lost in the noise of job listings, recruiter emails, and well-meaning advice from others. When your work aligns with your values, even challenging days have a sense of direction. When it doesn't, even well-paid jobs can feel like slow suffocation.

Take a moment to think about what truly matters to you in a workplace. Do you crave autonomy—the freedom to make decisions and shape your projects? Do you value collaboration and being part of a team that feels like a community? Do you need stability and structure to do your best work, or do you thrive in environments that are constantly evolving?

Many people end up in roles that clash with their values simply because they never identified those values in the first place. They accept offers based on salary alone, or prestige, or convenience, only to find themselves restless and discontent months later. When your daily reality contradicts your core values, something inside you begins to resist. You may feel stuck, uninspired, or strangely exhausted even when everything looks "fine" from the outside.

This isn't weakness. It's a signal. Your values are trying to speak to you.

For example, if integrity is a deeply held value and you find yourself in a company culture where cutting corners is encouraged, you'll feel a constant, quiet tension. If creativity fuels you but your role demands rigid conformity, your energy will drain over time. If you value meaningful human connection but spend your days isolated behind a screen, the job may slowly erode your sense of self.

Values act as both anchor and filter. They keep you grounded in who you are, and they help you sift through opportunities with greater clarity. Instead of asking, *Can I do this job?* you begin asking, *Does this job fit the kind of life I want to build?*

This doesn't mean chasing a fantasy of the perfect company. No workplace is flawless. But when your values align with your work environment, challenges become more bearable. Sacrifices feel purposeful rather than soul-depleting. You can grow without losing yourself.

It's also worth noting that your values may have evolved since the last time you thought seriously about your career. What mattered to you five years ago may not be what matters most now. Perhaps you once prioritized rapid growth but now crave balance. Perhaps financial security was your top concern, but now impact and meaning matter more. The job search is the perfect moment to take stock of those shifts—not with judgment, but with honesty.

You can test your alignment with values by imagining daily life in a potential role, not just the title on your résumé. Picture the meetings, the communication style, the pace, the kind of decisions you'd be involved in. Ask yourself whether those things would feed or deplete your energy. Sometimes, a job sounds exciting in theory but contradicts your deeper values in practice.

This stage of clarity is empowering because it turns the job search from a reactive scramble into a deliberate process. Instead of waiting for companies to pick you, you're picking them too. You're evaluating, not just being evaluated. That shift alone changes your posture, your tone, and your confidence.

When you align your values with your career, you also reduce the likelihood of burnout. Burnout isn't just about workload. It's about misalignment—working hard at something that doesn't feel meaningful. When your values and work are in harmony, effort feels purposeful, and even long hours don't hollow you out in the same way.

In interviews, values become one of your most powerful tools. When you can articulate what you stand for—not as slogans, but as lived principles—you attract the right kind of employers. You make it easier for the right doors to open and for the wrong ones to close.

This isn't about being idealistic. It's about being strategic. Your career isn't a single transaction; it's a long-term investment of your time, energy, and identity. Values ensure you invest wisely.

As you end this section, remember that clarity of purpose, awareness of strengths, and alignment with values aren't just exercises—they are the bedrock of everything that comes next. Before the résumés, before the interviews, before the negotiations, this inner work shapes how you show up. It's what turns a job search from a desperate chase into a confident, deliberate journey.

When you're rooted in who you are, the noise of the market doesn't control you. You stop moving like a leaf in the wind and start moving like someone who knows exactly where they're headed. And that clarity—quiet, steady, unshakable—will be the most powerful asset you carry with you in the weeks ahead.

Chapter 2: Building a Personal Narrative That Stands Out

2.1 Turning Your Story into a Strategy

When most people prepare for a job search, they think about polishing their résumé, updating their LinkedIn profile, or memorizing clever answers for interviews. What they often overlook is something far more powerful: the story that holds all of these elements together. A personal narrative is not a gimmick or a marketing trick. It's the thread that connects where you've been to where you want to go. When done well, it gives shape and meaning to your professional journey and makes you unforgettable in a sea of similar candidates.

But let's be clear: building a personal narrative is not about manufacturing some polished fairy tale. It's not about pretending your path has been linear, flawless, or perfectly calculated. In fact, some of the most compelling stories come from paths that have been winding, unexpected, or even messy. Employers and hiring managers don't need perfection—they crave authenticity. They want to understand how your experiences, decisions, and growth fit together into a coherent picture. A strong narrative allows them to do that quickly and clearly.

Every person has a story, but not everyone learns how to tell it well. Many candidates fall into one of two traps. The first is underselling themselves, reducing their journey to a dry list of roles and responsibilities. The second is overcomplicating their story, drowning the listener in irrelevant details and losing the thread. The key lies somewhere in between: being both specific and intentional, weaving the details of your past into a larger vision for your future.

The first step in crafting your personal narrative is understanding that your career isn't a collection of random jobs—it's a trajectory. Even if it has taken unexpected turns, there's a logic to it. Maybe you've followed your curiosity, maybe you've adapted to opportunities, or maybe you've reinvented yourself entirely. No matter the shape of your journey, it contains a pattern, and that pattern is your anchor.

To find it, start by stepping back and looking at your professional history with a storyteller's eye. Think about what motivated your transitions between roles. Was it the search for new challenges? The desire to learn something different? A shift in personal priorities? A need to align your work with your values? When you view your path through motivations rather than titles, a deeper structure begins to emerge.

Let's imagine someone who began in customer service, moved into marketing, and is now seeking a role in community engagement. On paper, that might look scattered. But with a well-crafted narrative, that same person can articulate a clear through line: a commitment to communication, connection, and creating positive experiences for people. Instead of a résumé filled with unrelated jobs, what the interviewer hears is a story of consistent focus and evolving expertise.

The power of a personal narrative also lies in your ability to give context. Job titles rarely tell the full story of what you actually did or learned. Maybe you were "Administrative Assistant," but in reality, you streamlined workflows, coordinated projects, solved problems no one else wanted to tackle, and became the person everyone relied on. Without a narrative, that experience gets buried under a generic job description. With a narrative, it becomes proof of your leadership, resourcefulness, and strategic thinking.

Your story also needs to communicate direction. Employers don't just want to know where you've been—they want to understand where you're headed. If your story ends at the past, it becomes a memoir. But if it points toward the future, it becomes a strategy. That's why it's essential to connect your past experiences to the kind of role you're now pursuing. Don't leave that connection for someone else to figure out. Show it to them. Draw the line yourself.

A well-structured personal narrative contains three essential movements: origin, evolution, and vision. The origin is how your journey began—not necessarily your very first job, but the point where the story makes sense to start. The evolution is the arc of growth, learning, and decisions that have shaped your professional identity. The vision is where all of this is leading. When you tell your story in this way, you transform your résumé from a flat timeline into a meaningful arc.

This doesn't mean rehearsing a monologue or forcing a script into every conversation. A narrative is not a rigid speech—it's a flexible framework. You should be able to adapt it depending on the context: the version you tell in a cover letter might emphasize one aspect, while the one you share in an interview might highlight another. But at its core, it should remain anchored in the same coherent truth.

To craft this framework, reflect on the pivotal moments in your journey. These are the transitions, challenges, or turning points that taught you something significant or clarified your direction. Maybe it was the first time you led a project, or the moment you realized you wanted to change industries. Maybe it was a setback that forced you to grow. These moments are powerful because they give your story texture. They make it human.

It's tempting to gloss over difficulties, but challenges often shape the most compelling parts of a narrative. If you changed careers after a layoff, if you went back to school mid-career, if you started over in a new field, these aren't weaknesses—they're proof of resilience and clarity. Employers respect candidates who can own their story with honesty and confidence.

But crafting a narrative isn't only about looking backward. It's also about defining what you want moving forward. This is where many job seekers falter. They can describe their past in detail but become vague when asked, "Where do you see yourself going?" or "Why this role?" Without a clear narrative, answers to those questions sound hesitant. With a narrative, they sound like a natural next step.

Think of your story as a bridge between your past and your future. On one side stands everything you've done—the experiences, skills, and lessons learned. On the other side is the vision you're moving toward. The narrative is the structure that connects the two, making the leap believable not just to an employer, but to yourself.

It's also important to remember that your story is not defined by your job titles. It's defined by the impact you've had and the person you've become through those experiences. Two people with the same job title can have entirely different narratives because what they contributed, learned, and prioritized was different. Your job is to find that personal angle.

An authentic personal narrative doesn't sound like a sales pitch. It doesn't rely on corporate jargon or memorized phrases. It sounds like a clear, confident explanation of why your journey makes sense and why your next step is a natural continuation of it. It should make an interviewer think, *Of course. This person fits.*

Another important aspect is owning the transitions in your story. People often feel embarrassed by gaps, career shifts, or nontraditional paths. But those very elements can be your advantage if you frame them correctly. A gap can signal intentional reflection or personal growth. A shift can demonstrate adaptability and courage. Employers are far less concerned about "perfect" paths than they are about people who can clearly explain their choices.

This is why storytelling is such a powerful tool. When you don't tell your story, others fill in the blanks for you. When you do tell it—truthfully, strategically, and confidently—you shape how people perceive you. You guide the conversation. You take ownership of your narrative instead of letting it be defined by assumptions.

Building a personal narrative also has a subtle but profound psychological effect. When you hear yourself telling your story with clarity, something shifts inside you. You stop feeling like someone stumbling through an uncertain transition and start feeling like the author of your own career. That mindset alone changes the way you write emails, walk into interviews, and evaluate opportunities.

Finally, remember that a narrative is a living thing. It doesn't have to be perfect or final. It will evolve as you evolve. The version you tell today might look different six months from now, and that's a sign of growth. What matters is that it feels real to you now.

This chapter isn't about teaching you how to perform. It's about helping you reclaim your story and wield it with purpose. When you can express who you are, where you've been, and where you're going in a way that feels both honest and strategic, everything else—the résumé, the cover letter, the interview—falls into place more naturally.

A job search without a narrative feels like shouting into a void. A job search with a narrative feels like opening doors with intention. And once you learn how to shape and share your story, you stop waiting for someone else to recognize your value. You start *showing* it.

2.2 Identifying the Defining Moments in Your Journey

Every meaningful personal narrative has turning points—moments that shape the trajectory of your life and career in ways that are both subtle and profound. These are not always glamorous milestones like promotions or awards. More often, they are moments of realization, challenge, or transition. They're the instances where something shifted: your understanding of yourself, your sense of direction, or your view of what matters. Identifying these defining moments is what transforms your story from a list of job titles into a narrative that carries weight, texture, and authenticity.

Think back to the earliest stages of your career or even further, to the times before you officially entered the workforce. What drove you toward the path you took? Sometimes, these early decisions are rooted in passion. Sometimes, they're shaped by necessity. Sometimes, they emerge from unexpected opportunities. All of those reasons matter. What's important is recognizing the threads that connect them.

A defining moment doesn't have to be dramatic. It can be quiet but deeply formative. It could be the first time someone trusted you with responsibility you didn't think you were ready for, and you rose to the occasion. It could be the moment you realized that a certain kind of work didn't fit you anymore, even if you had invested years in it. It might be a project that challenged every assumption you held about your abilities, or a setback that forced you to see yourself differently.

For many people, these defining moments don't look like victories from the outside. Some of the most powerful stories begin in failure. A business that didn't succeed, a role that didn't feel right, a rejection that hurt more than expected—these experiences often hold the seeds of transformation. When you look closely at them, you'll find they taught you something crucial: resilience, clarity, courage, humility, or the importance of trusting your instincts.

Revisiting these moments requires honesty. It's tempting to gloss over the uncomfortable parts of our stories, to package everything in a neat and polished way. But a narrative built only on triumphs feels hollow. Real stories have complexity. They contain highs and lows, moments of certainty and moments of doubt. The key is not to dwell on the difficulties but to understand what they reveal about your character and direction.

Let's imagine someone who worked for several years in a corporate role that never felt quite right. The defining moment for that person might not be the day they landed the job but the day they admitted to themselves that it wasn't the right fit. That decision—to acknowledge discomfort and take ownership of their future—is a turning point. It marks a shift from passivity to agency. And in the context of a job search, that moment can become a powerful part of their story: not as a failure, but as a declaration of self-awareness and courage.

Another example might be a period of rapid growth. Perhaps there was a project that forced you to develop skills you didn't know you had, a situation that stretched you in uncomfortable but ultimately rewarding ways. That moment, when you rose to the challenge, reveals your adaptability and capacity to learn. It becomes a living example of your strengths in action—not something you merely claim but something you've proven through experience.

Sometimes defining moments happen outside formal work settings. A volunteer experience, a side project, a personal challenge, or even a period of travel can reshape how you view your career. These experiences matter because they contribute to your identity as a professional. They may have taught you leadership, resourcefulness, empathy, or creative problem-solving. Just because something didn't appear on your résumé doesn't mean it isn't part of your story.

When identifying these moments, it's useful to pay attention to emotional weight. Which experiences stay with you, even years later? Which ones made you feel something powerful—whether that was exhilaration, fear, pride, or clarity? Strong emotions are often signposts pointing to moments that shaped you. They are the raw material of your narrative.

Defining moments are also about choices. A career isn't shaped just by what happens to you but by how you respond to what happens. If you chose to pivot careers, if you decided to stand up for your principles, if you stepped into a leadership role before you felt ready, those decisions reveal something meaningful about who you are. They're evidence of your values and your capacity to take action.

It's also worth noting that what feels ordinary to you may be extraordinary to someone else. People often underestimate their own defining moments because they lived them day by day. But to an employer hearing your story for the first time, those moments can be powerful and memorable. What matters is not how impressive they look on paper but how clearly you can articulate their impact on who you are today.

Crafting your narrative around these moments doesn't mean exaggerating or dramatizing them. It means honoring their significance and weaving them into a coherent story. When you can explain why a particular moment mattered—how it changed your perspective, shaped your skills, or set you on a new path—you give your story emotional depth. That depth is what makes it resonate with others.

Finally, remember that your defining moments don't need to follow a neat chronological order. Some may come early in your life, others may be recent. Some may represent turning points, while others may be quiet realizations that took time to crystallize. What ties them together is their role in shaping your identity and direction.

When you can name these moments and understand their meaning, you gain a powerful tool. You no longer approach interviews or networking conversations as someone trying to justify a list of jobs. You step into them as someone with a story—a real story that reveals not just what you've done, but who you are.

2.3 Shaping a Cohesive and Authentic Narrative

Once you've identified the defining moments of your journey, the next step is to weave them into a cohesive and authentic narrative. This is where your story begins to take shape as something more than a collection of anecdotes. It becomes a strategic, structured way to present yourself that resonates with clarity, confidence, and credibility.

Cohesion doesn't mean forcing your experiences into a perfectly linear plot. Very few careers follow a straight line. What matters is the thread—the underlying theme that ties your experiences together. This thread might be a value, a skill, a motivation, or a way of approaching challenges. Perhaps your story is one of curiosity driving constant growth. Perhaps it's about problem-solving and creating order out of complexity. Or perhaps it's about communication, connection, or innovation. Whatever it is, identifying this thread is what allows your story to feel whole, even if your path has been diverse.

To find that thread, step back and look at the defining moments you've collected. Ask yourself what connects them. Was it a repeated decision to step into leadership? A recurring desire to work on meaningful projects? A consistent tendency to bridge gaps between people or disciplines? The patterns that emerge here will form the backbone of your narrative.

A cohesive narrative isn't about pretending that everything was perfectly planned. It's about showing that your journey has meaning. Even detours, setbacks, or pivots can make sense when they're placed in context. If you switched industries, for example, don't apologize for it—explain why it made sense at that moment, what it taught you, and how it contributes to the value you bring today.

Authenticity is just as crucial as structure. A narrative that sounds rehearsed or artificial will fall flat, no matter how well organized it is. The power of a personal story lies in its humanity. Speak about your journey the way you would to someone genuinely interested in understanding you, not as if you're reciting a pitch. This doesn't mean oversharing or revealing every personal detail. It means choosing your words carefully so they reflect your real voice.

One of the most effective ways to achieve authenticity is to focus on clarity rather than performance. Don't try to sound impressive; try to sound real. When you explain why a certain moment shaped you, speak from the perspective of someone who lived it, not someone trying to sell it. That honesty is disarming and memorable. Employers meet countless candidates who present a polished façade but few who present a coherent, human story.

A well-shaped narrative also has rhythm. It doesn't linger too long on any one moment, and it moves naturally from past to present to future. Your past gives context, your present shows your readiness, and your future conveys your vision. When those three elements align, your story has momentum. It carries the listener along with it.

For example, imagine someone who started their career as a teacher, transitioned into corporate training, and now wants to work in learning and development for a tech company. Their narrative doesn't need to apologize for the shifts. Instead, it might sound something like this: they discovered early on that they were passionate about helping people grow, found new ways to apply that passion in different contexts, and are now ready to bring that experience to a larger, faster-moving environment. The thread is clear. The story makes sense.

A cohesive narrative also prepares you for the unpredictable moments in interviews—the questions that don't quite fit a script. When you have a strong story, you don't need to memorize answers. You simply adapt your narrative to the question. It becomes the foundation from which all your responses flow.

Authenticity also requires embracing the imperfections in your journey. If there were gaps, transitions, or unconventional moves, own them. When you can explain those moments calmly and clearly, they lose their power to undermine you. They become part of your unique path. Employers don't expect a flawless story—they expect an honest one.

Another subtle but important part of shaping your narrative is emotional resonance. People may forget facts and figures, but they remember how you make them feel. When your story carries conviction, when it reflects genuine reflection and self-awareness, it creates a quiet trust. And trust is what turns an interview from a transaction into a connection.

This connection isn't about being theatrical or overselling. It's about speaking from a grounded place, where your experiences and intentions align. When you believe in your own story, others are more likely to believe in it too. That's why this work matters—it doesn't just convince others; it strengthens your own sense of identity.

A cohesive and authentic narrative gives you more than a way to answer "Tell me about yourself." It gives you a foundation for your entire job search. It shapes how you write your résumé, how you approach networking conversations, how you tailor your cover letters, and how you negotiate. It gives you direction. It allows you to speak from clarity rather than improvisation.

Most importantly, it turns your career journey into something you own. Instead of feeling like your past is a puzzle you're constantly trying to explain, it becomes the story you stand on. That sense of ownership changes the way you show up in every interaction.

By the time you finish shaping your narrative, you should be able to express it confidently and comfortably. It doesn't need to be long or embellished. It just needs to be yours—cohesive, honest, and alive. And when it is, the people listening to you will sense it. They won't just hear the facts of your career; they'll understand the person behind them. And that is where opportunities truly begin to open.

Chapter 3: Crafting an Application That Opens Doors

3.1 The Art of Making a First Impression

Long before you shake hands with an interviewer or look into a hiring manager's eyes, your application has already spoken for you. In fact, in most cases, it's the only thing standing between you and the next step in the hiring process. The résumé, the cover letter, the LinkedIn profile, the portfolio—these are not mere formalities. They're your introduction, your first impression, and in a crowded marketplace, they often determine whether your story gets heard at all.

Too many people treat applications like administrative tasks. They fill in templates, recycle the same résumé for different roles, and hope that something sticks. But employers and recruiters read dozens—sometimes hundreds—of applications for a single opening. They don't remember those who blend into the background. They remember the ones whose materials tell a clear, compelling story from the very first glance. That's why crafting a strong application isn't about decoration or buzzwords. It's about clarity, precision, and the subtle art of making someone stop, pay attention, and want to know more.

A first impression in writing functions differently than one in person. In a conversation, you can adjust your tone, your body language, your pacing. On paper, you have no second chance. The words and structure you choose either create an immediate sense of alignment—or they don't. This is why an effective application isn't just a list of past experiences but a carefully constructed narrative bridge between your history and the role you're pursuing.

Imagine, for a moment, being the person on the other side of the process. A hiring manager opens a résumé. Within the first ten seconds, they're asking themselves a set of unspoken questions: Does this candidate seem relevant to the role? Do they appear focused or scattered? Can I quickly understand what they offer? Is there something here that makes them stand out from the dozens of others? If your materials answer these questions smoothly, you already have an advantage. If they don't, your story may never even reach the interview stage.

The essence of a powerful first impression lies in intentionality. Every word, every line, every choice in your application should have a purpose. That doesn't mean it needs to be flashy or extravagant. In fact, simplicity often speaks louder than excess. What matters is that the person reading it can immediately sense the clarity behind it. When someone opens your résumé, they should not have to work hard to understand your value. It should be evident from the very first section.

This kind of clarity begins with how you present yourself—not just what you've done, but how you frame it. Many candidates make the mistake of treating their résumé as a historical archive, listing every job and responsibility they've ever had. But a résumé is not a biography; it's a curated snapshot of your professional identity, designed to highlight what matters most for the role at hand. The goal is not to overwhelm with volume but to communicate impact.

Think of your application as a handshake that happens before you enter the room. A strong handshake conveys confidence, respect, and readiness. A weak or rushed one communicates uncertainty. The same is true here. A well-structured résumé with a clear narrative tells an employer that you understand your own value and can express it concisely. A scattered or vague application tells them you're still figuring it out.

Of course, your résumé is just one piece of this introduction. A thoughtful cover letter can bring your story to life in a way the résumé can't. Where the résumé shows what you've done, the cover letter explains why it matters. Where the résumé is structured, the letter allows for nuance and voice. But for it to work, it must be personal, not generic. A template copied and pasted into dozens of applications is easy to spot—and easy to ignore. A letter that reflects genuine engagement with the role and company, on the other hand, creates a spark of connection.

This doesn't mean you need to craft an entirely new letter for every application, but it does mean each one should feel specific. Addressing why you're drawn to the company, how your background connects to their mission, and what value you can bring to their team can transform a routine letter into something memorable. Employers can sense when you've written something with intention. They can also sense when you haven't.

But beyond the content itself, presentation matters. Your application materials should be clean, readable, and easy to follow. If someone has to hunt for the information that matters, they won't. If your formatting is messy or inconsistent, it creates a subtle but real impression of carelessness. Clarity of presentation signals clarity of thought. It shows that you respect the reader's time.

What makes a first impression powerful isn't perfection; it's coherence. Your résumé, cover letter, LinkedIn profile, and any portfolio you might have should tell the same story from different angles. A common mistake is treating each piece as separate, creating small inconsistencies that weaken the overall impact. When your story is consistent across all platforms, you project a sense of stability and confidence. It's like meeting someone who introduces themselves the same way every time—not because they're rehearsed, but because they know who they are.

To understand the weight of a first impression, consider how little time recruiters actually spend reviewing applications. Research shows that initial résumé scans often last under thirty seconds. That's the window you have to create clarity and intrigue. That doesn't mean you should try to cram everything into the top half of the page in desperation. It means you need to be deliberate about what information goes where, how it flows, and what it communicates.

Think of this process as setting a stage. When a curtain rises at a theater, the first scene doesn't reveal everything, but it sets the tone. It makes the audience decide whether to lean forward or drift away. Your résumé's top section is your opening scene. Your cover letter is the monologue that draws them in. Your online presence is the backdrop that confirms the story is real. Each element works together to create a single impression: credible, intentional, and compelling.

A common misconception is that the most impressive résumé wins. In truth, it's often the clearest résumé that wins. A résumé packed with jargon, complex formatting, or vague achievements is harder to connect with. But a résumé that clearly conveys a candidate's strengths and trajectory invites the reader in. It allows them to imagine you in the role.

This is where strategy comes into play. A well-crafted application isn't about trying to be everything to everyone. It's about alignment. You want your materials to show, without forcing the point, why you're a natural fit for the role you're applying to. That alignment doesn't need to scream—it just needs to hum beneath the surface, subtly guiding the reader toward the conclusion that you belong in the conversation.

The most effective applications are built not on desperation but on confidence. They don't say, "Please consider me." They say, "Here's who I am and why I can help you solve the problems you care about." That shift in tone is almost invisible, but it's profound. It's the difference between knocking timidly on a door and walking up to it with the calm certainty that you have something valuable to offer.

This doesn't mean exaggerating or pretending to be more than you are. In fact, exaggeration almost always backfires. Recruiters can sense when someone is trying too hard to sell themselves. Authenticity has its own quiet weight. When you can communicate your story truthfully but strategically—highlighting the experiences that matter, clarifying the direction you're headed, and showing why this role fits into that path—you create a presence even before you enter the room.

Crafting this kind of first impression takes time. It requires reflection, editing, and a willingness to refine. But once you build it, it becomes a powerful ally throughout your search. Every time you send out your application, it will work for you—not as a static document, but as a compelling invitation to learn more about the person behind it.

What often surprises people is how this clarity changes not only how employers see them but how they see themselves. When your application truly reflects your story, it reinforces your confidence. It reminds you of your trajectory, your strengths, and your value. That quiet self-assurance radiates through your writing, your interviews, and your interactions.

In the end, your first impression is not just about getting noticed. It's about setting the tone for everything that follows. It's about creating a foundation of trust and curiosity strong enough to carry you to the next stage. And when that first impression is crafted with care, precision, and authenticity, it can open doors that might otherwise have remained closed.

3.2 The Resume as a Strategic Document

A résumé is often described as a summary of your professional history, but that description falls short of its real function. A résumé isn't just a catalog of jobs you've held—it's a strategic document designed to guide the reader toward a specific conclusion: that you are the right person for this role. When written with intention, it becomes more than a list of experiences; it's a carefully structured argument, a story told in precise and economical language, designed to open a door.

The first step in transforming your résumé from a static sheet into a strategic tool is to stop treating it as a personal archive. You are not obligated to include every job, project, or qualification you've ever accumulated. The goal is not to overwhelm the reader with volume but to direct their attention toward what matters most in the context of the position you're pursuing. This means making deliberate choices—what to include, what to emphasize, what to leave out. Strategy is about focus, and a focused résumé is far more powerful than a comprehensive one.

A strategic résumé begins with a clear sense of purpose. Ask yourself: What story am I telling? Where is this story leading? Every section of your résumé should point toward a central narrative about who you are as a professional and why you're a strong fit for this opportunity. Even if your background spans multiple industries, roles, or experiences, your résumé should pull those threads together into a single, coherent impression.

The top of your résumé carries the most weight. This is where the reader decides, consciously or not, whether to keep reading. A well-written opening section—whether it's a succinct summary statement or a carefully framed professional profile—serves as your first handshake. It should immediately communicate your value, your area of focus, and the direction of your career. This is not the place for vague language. Empty phrases like "results-oriented professional" or "highly motivated team player" say nothing specific. Clarity and precision, on the other hand, show confidence and give the reader a reason to pay attention.

Many people underestimate how much structure shapes perception. The way you order your experiences can either clarify your trajectory or make it feel disjointed. If you've had a straightforward path, reverse chronological order often works best—it highlights your most recent and relevant experiences first. But if your path includes shifts or nontraditional moves, structure becomes even more important. You may need to group experiences thematically or emphasize skills and accomplishments over job titles. What matters is how well the structure supports the story you want to tell.

A strategic résumé also prioritizes impact over activity. Listing responsibilities is not enough. Hiring managers don't just want to know what you were *supposed* to do—they want to know what you actually *achieved*. Instead of saying you "managed projects," explain the outcomes of those projects. Instead of noting you "led a team," clarify how that leadership made a difference. Numbers, results, and concrete examples give weight to your claims. They help the reader imagine you producing results for them.

But strategy doesn't end with achievements. Context matters too. A strong résumé subtly communicates not only what you did, but why it matters. For example, if you introduced a new process at work, it's more powerful to explain that it saved time or improved accuracy than to simply state that you "created a process." By linking your actions to tangible outcomes, you help the reader understand the value you bring without having to spell it out explicitly.

Another element that distinguishes a strategic résumé from a generic one is intentional language. Every line should carry meaning. Words that are vague, inflated, or interchangeable with hundreds of other résumés weaken the impact. Words that are sharp, specific, and grounded in real contribution stand out. This doesn't mean trying to sound overly formal or academic; it means choosing language that is clean, direct, and purposeful.

Length is often misunderstood. A résumé should be as long as it needs to be—but no longer. For many people, this means a single page, especially in the earlier stages of their career. For those with extensive experience, two pages may be appropriate. What matters more than page count is the economy of expression. Every line should earn its place. If something doesn't support the story you're trying to tell, it doesn't belong.

Design plays a subtle but important role as well. While content always matters more than aesthetics, presentation affects how easily the reader can absorb your message. A résumé cluttered with dense paragraphs or inconsistent formatting creates friction. A clean, well-structured layout, on the other hand, invites the eye to follow along. White space is not wasted space—it's what makes your content breathable and digestible. The visual clarity of your résumé reflects the mental clarity you bring to your work.

A truly strategic résumé also considers the way hiring works today. Many companies use applicant tracking systems to scan résumés before a human ever sees them. That doesn't mean stuffing your document with keywords like a desperate trick. It means understanding the language of the role you're applying for and ensuring your résumé speaks it naturally. If a job posting repeatedly emphasizes "cross-functional collaboration," and that reflects your experience, your résumé should reflect it in clear, natural language.

But while technology plays a role, it's still humans who make the final decisions. That's why your résumé should not sound like it was written for a machine. It should sound like it was written for someone intelligent, busy, and curious—a person who wants to understand your value in a matter of seconds. A strategic résumé balances both worlds: clear enough to pass through filters, human enough to create interest.

Above all, a résumé should feel like *you*. Not in a casual or informal sense, but in the sense that it reflects your strengths, your focus, and your voice. If your résumé could be swapped with someone else's without losing its meaning, it's too generic. If it makes someone reading it want to meet the person behind the page, you've achieved your goal.

What sets a strategic résumé apart isn't just polish—it's intention. It doesn't try to tell everything. It tells the right things, in the right way, to the right people. It guides the reader gently but firmly toward the conclusion that you are a strong candidate. It opens the door, not by shouting, but by being clear, confident, and memorable.

3.3 The Cover Letter as a Personal Bridge

If the résumé is the anchor of your application, the cover letter is the bridge between your story and the employer's world. It's your opportunity to shift from static facts to living narrative, to explain why your experience matters in this specific context. When done well, a cover letter is not a repetition of your résumé. It's the piece that gives it shape, depth, and direction.

Unfortunately, most cover letters are written as formal obligations. Candidates recycle the same polite phrases, express generic enthusiasm, and hope it will pass unnoticed. But in a competitive job market, a letter like that does more harm than good. It signals indifference. A thoughtful, well-crafted letter, on the other hand, can change how your entire application is perceived.

A cover letter works best when it answers an unspoken question in the hiring manager's mind: *Why you? Why here? Why now?* It should offer a narrative that links your background to the company's needs, showing not just that you *can* do the job, but that you *want* to do it, and that your trajectory makes this opportunity a meaningful next step.

The tone of a strong cover letter is confident but not arrogant, personal but not casual. It should sound like a real human being speaking directly to another human being. That doesn't mean oversharing personal details or being overly emotional. It means writing with clarity, warmth, and intent.

One of the most common mistakes in cover letters is trying to restate the résumé. If your letter is just a rephrased list of your accomplishments, it adds nothing. Instead, use it to highlight the parts of your story that matter most for this specific role. Explain why those experiences are relevant. Share what drew you to this company. Show that you've taken the time to understand their work.

A powerful letter often has a subtle arc. It begins by establishing connection, moves through your relevant experience, and ends with a sense of forward momentum. It doesn't need to be long. In fact, brevity often makes it stronger. What matters is that every sentence has a purpose. A letter that meanders or drowns in vague statements will be skimmed and forgotten. A letter that speaks directly and intentionally will be remembered.

Specificity is your ally. Mentioning something meaningful about the company—a project, a value, a direction they're taking—shows that you're not sending out mass applications. It signals interest. More importantly, it gives you a way to connect your story to theirs. If you can show how your skills align with their needs, you create a sense of fit before the interview even happens.

But a cover letter isn't just about convincing the employer. It's also about grounding yourself. When you write a letter that genuinely reflects why you're pursuing this opportunity, it reminds you of your own direction. It reinforces your clarity. You're not just sending documents; you're initiating a conversation.

Many people fear sounding too forward or bold in their letters. But hiring managers are not looking for meekness—they're looking for clarity and confidence. A letter that clearly communicates, "Here's who I am, here's why I care about what you're doing, and here's why I'd be an asset to your team," stands out in a pile of vague pleasantries.

The language of a strong cover letter is simple and direct. It avoids buzzwords and inflated claims. It focuses on connection and alignment. It's not about proving you're perfect. It's about showing you're intentional.

When written well, a cover letter can also soften edges in your résumé. If you've made a career shift, if you're reentering the workforce, if there's something in your path that might raise questions, the letter allows you to explain it in your own words. This turns potential red flags into context. It turns uncertainty into narrative.

Equally important is the way a cover letter closes. Many people end with weak, perfunctory phrases that fade into the background. But a strong closing can linger. A clear, confident invitation to continue the conversation—a line that reaffirms your enthusiasm and leaves a sense of energy—can tilt the balance in your favor.

It's worth remembering that not every hiring manager reads every letter. But the ones who do tend to care deeply about finding candidates who fit not just the job, but the culture and mission. A strong letter speaks to them directly. It shows them that you're not just qualified—you're engaged.

Writing a cover letter is less about formalities and more about intention. It's about extending a hand across the distance between your story and theirs. It's your chance to speak in a voice that is both professional and personal. And when you do that with clarity and sincerity, your application stops being just another document in a stack. It becomes a story that someone wants to hear more of.

In a world where so much of job searching feels automated, the cover letter remains one of the last places where your voice can break through the noise. It's where a résumé becomes human. It's where an application becomes a conversation. And when used strategically, it can be the element that turns a maybe into a yes.

Chapter 4: Mastering the Art of Networking

4.1 Reframing Networking: From Transaction to Connection

For many job seekers, the word "networking" brings up a mix of discomfort and resistance. It can feel forced, opportunistic, or even insincere—a room full of strangers exchanging business cards, rehearsed smiles, and half-forgotten conversations. It's often associated with awkward events, superficial interactions, and a sense of pretending to be more "together" than you feel. But this image of networking is not only limiting; it's fundamentally misleading. Real networking isn't about collecting contacts or forcing conversations. It's about building genuine connections that have meaning, trust, and mutual value.

If your experience of networking so far has been draining, it may be because you've approached it with a transactional mindset—the idea that networking is about getting something from someone. That approach rarely works, not because people are selfish, but because human beings have a natural sensitivity to authenticity. When someone approaches a conversation with the intent to extract, it shows. People feel it. And that invisible signal can turn what might have been a meaningful connection into a closed door.

Reframing networking begins with a fundamental shift in how you see it. Instead of viewing it as a means to an end, start seeing it as a way to build relationships that might open doors in their own time. The most powerful professional connections aren't born out of perfectly timed requests; they emerge from genuine conversations, shared interests, and mutual respect. When you stop trying to "network" in the stereotypical sense and start focusing on connecting, the process becomes less about strategy and more about authenticity.

This shift isn't just psychological. It has practical consequences. A person who approaches networking with openness and curiosity rather than a rigid agenda will naturally attract more meaningful conversations. They'll also be remembered more vividly because sincerity stands out in professional spaces. Networking, at its best, isn't a performance—it's a dialogue.

To understand this, it helps to recognize how opportunities actually flow through networks. Most people imagine opportunities come from influential gatekeepers—top executives, recruiters, or industry stars. In reality, many life-changing connections happen through what sociologists call "weak ties": people on the periphery of your immediate circle. A friend of a friend. A former colleague. Someone you met at a conference two years ago. These weak ties are powerful because they extend your reach into new spaces, exposing you to perspectives, industries, and chances you wouldn't have encountered otherwise.

But weak ties only work when they're built on real connection. And real connection requires you to show up as a person, not as a walking résumé. This is where many job seekers stumble. They approach conversations with a subtle undercurrent of urgency: *What can this person do for me? How can they help me get what I want?* But strong networks grow in the opposite direction. When you approach someone with curiosity—when you genuinely want to understand their work, their interests, their path—you create an opening for something real to grow.

Networking isn't about quantity; it's about quality. A handful of genuine relationships will carry more weight than a hundred superficial contacts. It's not about how many business cards you can collect, how many people follow you online, or how many messages you send. It's about the depth and sincerity of your interactions.

Many people also make the mistake of thinking networking is something they should do only when they need something—especially a job. But the best time to build a network isn't during a job search. It's before you need it. That doesn't mean you can't begin now if you're in that position. It simply means your approach should be centered not on urgency, but on connection. Relationships built under pressure tend to be fragile. Relationships built on genuine interest tend to last.

One of the biggest barriers people face when networking is the fear of being a burden. They hesitate to reach out because they worry about taking up someone's time or seeming needy. But when your intention is grounded in curiosity, respect, and generosity, you're not a burden—you're someone engaging in a human exchange. Most people actually like to talk about their work, their path, and their perspective. When you give them space to share that without immediately turning it into a request, you create a space where trust can grow.

Equally important is shifting how you see your own value. Networking isn't a one-way street where one person has power and the other is trying to get a favor. You have something to offer, too—perspective, energy, insight, introductions, support. Even if you're early in your career or changing fields, your curiosity, respect, and willingness to engage can be just as valuable as a polished résumé. People remember how you make them feel more than they remember the details of what you said.

Another misconception is that networking requires being extroverted or socially dominant. It doesn't. Some of the most powerful connectors are thoughtful listeners. They make people feel heard. They ask questions others don't. They create conversations that are slower, quieter, but far more meaningful. If networking feels performative to you, that may be a sign you're trying to imitate someone else's style. You don't need to mimic the loudest voice in the room. Your own way of connecting is enough.

This shift in perspective also changes how you experience networking events—whether in person or virtual. Instead of seeing them as high-stakes auditions, think of them as opportunities to meet people whose paths may cross with yours in unpredictable but meaningful ways. Not every conversation has to lead to a job offer. Most won't. But every conversation is a chance to learn, to grow, to exchange perspectives. Over time, those conversations build a web of trust that can support your career in ways you can't yet see.

A useful way to think about networking is to view it as planting seeds. Some will sprout quickly. Others may take months or years. Some may never grow at all. That's okay. The point isn't to control the outcome. The point is to cultivate an ecosystem of genuine connections. Opportunities often come from unexpected directions, and what feels like a casual conversation today might become a turning point tomorrow.

The best networkers are those who understand reciprocity—not as a calculated transaction, but as a natural part of human connection. They give as much as they receive. They share information, offer introductions, celebrate others' successes, and stay present. When you become the kind of person who supports others without an immediate expectation of return, people remember you not as someone who asked for a favor, but as someone they trust.

It's also important to understand that networking isn't limited to formal spaces. Many people imagine it as cocktail receptions, conferences, or LinkedIn outreach. In reality, networking happens everywhere—on walks with friends, at workshops, online forums, in shared interest groups, and in casual conversations. Some of the most valuable connections are born in spaces where neither person is trying to "network." This is why living and working with openness matters. When you carry genuine curiosity into your daily interactions, networking becomes less of a chore and more of a natural extension of how you move through the world.

A reimagined approach to networking also helps ease the anxiety that so often comes with job searches. Instead of feeling like you're begging strangers for help, you begin to see yourself as part of a larger web of people, each with something to offer and something to learn. That mindset is not only more sustainable but also more empowering.

In this context, follow-ups and ongoing contact stop feeling like transactions and start feeling like conversations. When you follow up with someone after a meaningful exchange, you're not pestering them. You're continuing a relationship. When you share something relevant or express gratitude for their time, you're reinforcing trust. Networking isn't built in a single interaction—it's built in the spaces between them, the ongoing connections that evolve over time.

One of the most powerful shifts you can make is to view networking less as "finding people who can help me" and more as "building relationships with people I respect." When your outreach is rooted in respect rather than need, it changes your language, your tone, and the energy of the interaction. And people respond to that difference.

Reframing networking also means accepting that not every interaction will lead to something concrete—and that's okay. The value of networking isn't measured only in job offers. It's measured in the richness of your connections, the insights you gain, the way your perspective broadens. Those intangible benefits often end up being just as important as tangible outcomes.

Ultimately, networking is less about clever tactics and more about how you choose to show up in the world. When you approach it as an exercise in authentic connection—when you listen more than you speak, when you give more than you ask, when you nurture rather than extract—you stop dreading it. You begin to experience it as something natural, even meaningful.

And when you build your network from that place of authenticity, something remarkable happens: opportunities begin to find you. Not because you've perfected some secret strategy, but because people trust you, remember you, and want to work with you. That is the quiet power of connection. It doesn't shout, but it lasts.

4.2 Building Genuine Professional Relationships

If reframing networking is the first step, the next is learning how to build professional relationships that actually endure. It's easy to collect names, exchange pleasantries, or send out a flood of connection requests online. But those surface-level gestures rarely lead to anything meaningful. A real network is built on trust, familiarity, and shared understanding. And trust isn't built overnight—it grows gradually, through small and sincere interactions.

Many people assume professional relationships must always be formal and goal-oriented, but some of the most powerful professional connections emerge from simple, human conversations. A genuine relationship is not built on a transaction; it's built on a sense of mutual recognition. When two people connect because they see value in each other—not just what one can extract from the other—they create a foundation that can support opportunities in unpredictable ways.

The essence of building genuine professional relationships lies in showing up as your authentic self. That doesn't mean abandoning professionalism or sharing every detail of your personal life. It means being honest, curious, and fully present in your interactions. When someone senses that you are genuinely listening—not waiting to speak, not maneuvering to insert your pitch, but truly listening—they feel seen. And feeling seen is what makes people remember you.

Listening is often underestimated in networking, but it's one of the most powerful tools you have. People naturally open up to those who make space for them. When you take the time to ask real questions and genuinely care about the answers, the tone of the interaction changes. You stop being just another name on a list and become a person they associate with a meaningful moment.

Equally important is consistency. A single conversation can spark a connection, but relationships are forged in follow-through. That doesn't mean bombarding someone with messages. It means staying gently present. A quick note after an event, a shared article that reminded you of a conversation, a short message of encouragement when you see their professional updates—these small gestures build a bridge over time.

Professional relationships deepen when they aren't tied exclusively to immediate goals. If your interactions always revolve around asking for something, the connection becomes lopsided. But when you engage without expectation—when you show genuine interest in the other person's growth, ideas, or achievements—you build a foundation of mutual respect. Over time, this turns into trust.

One of the most overlooked ways to nurture these relationships is through generosity. This doesn't mean grand gestures or self-sacrifice. It can be as simple as sharing knowledge, introducing people to each other, or offering encouragement when someone is taking a leap. Generosity creates reciprocity, not because you demand it, but because human beings respond to sincerity. When you become someone who lifts others up, you become memorable.

It's also important to embrace the idea that professional relationships aren't meant to be forced. Not every conversation will lead to a strong connection, and that's perfectly natural. Just like in personal life, not everyone will be your person. The key is to focus your energy on the connections that feel real rather than trying to turn every interaction into a relationship.

Another misconception is that professional relationships have to be built only with people "above" you in the hierarchy—those who can offer opportunities. That kind of narrow thinking limits your possibilities. Some of the strongest networks are built laterally—with peers, collaborators, people growing alongside you. These relationships can evolve organically as your careers develop in parallel, often becoming the most valuable connections over time.

Authenticity in relationship-building also means being transparent about your intentions. You don't have to hide that you're looking for opportunities or trying to grow in your field. The difference lies in *how* you communicate that. When people sense that your interest in them is sincere—not just in what they can offer—you earn their respect. Respect is the true currency of professional relationships.

Another often-overlooked aspect is patience. In a culture that celebrates speed and instant results, it's easy to get frustrated when connections don't produce immediate outcomes. But the strongest networks work like slow-growing roots, invisible at first, then quietly supporting your growth when the time is right. You can't rush genuine trust. You can only cultivate it.

When building relationships, presence matters more than performance. You don't have to be the loudest voice in the room or the most charismatic person at an event. Showing up consistently, speaking with clarity, and listening with genuine curiosity will take you further than forced charm ever will.

In the digital age, it's also worth remembering that many professional relationships begin online. But an online connection doesn't become meaningful just because you've clicked "connect." Meaning grows when you engage thoughtfully—commenting on someone's work, congratulating their milestones, sharing insights that resonate. These are small acts, but over time, they accumulate. They show that you're not just a name on a list, but someone paying attention.

The key to building genuine professional relationships is understanding that the value of a network isn't measured in its size but in its depth. Ten real connections built on trust and respect will take you further than a hundred superficial contacts. Those real connections become allies, collaborators, mentors, and sometimes friends. They become part of the ecosystem that sustains your career.

At its core, building a professional relationship isn't so different from any meaningful human connection. It requires time, attention, honesty, and reciprocity. When you stop trying to engineer relationships and start allowing them to grow through authentic engagement, the pressure fades. You no longer feel like you're "networking." You're simply connecting.

And when your network is built on those kinds of relationships, something subtle but powerful happens: your professional life stops being a series of isolated job hunts and starts becoming an ongoing exchange with people who see you, trust you, and want to see you thrive.

4.3 Strategic Visibility Without Self-Promotion

One of the greatest misunderstandings about networking is the belief that being visible means being loud. People often assume they need to constantly promote themselves, push their achievements into every conversation, or turn every interaction into a personal advertisement. That kind of forced self-promotion is exhausting—not only for the person doing it but for everyone around them. True visibility works differently. It's quieter, more strategic, and ultimately more powerful.

Strategic visibility is not about shouting your accomplishments. It's about making your presence known in a way that feels natural, consistent, and rooted in your genuine value. It's the difference between someone trying to grab attention and someone whose contributions naturally attract it. When done well, visibility doesn't feel like self-promotion; it feels like participation.

The key to achieving this lies in shifting your focus from yourself to the value you bring into a space. People remember those who contribute thoughtfully. They remember insights shared at the right time, questions that reveal depth, and small gestures that make conversations richer. When you focus on contributing, visibility follows naturally. You become someone people think of not because you're constantly talking about yourself, but because you've become part of the fabric of the conversation.

This applies equally to in-person and digital interactions. In the physical world, visibility can be as simple as showing up—consistently attending events, participating in discussions, and engaging with others in a way that feels real. In the digital world, it means contributing to the spaces where your industry gathers. That might mean sharing perspectives, reflecting on trends, offering useful resources, or amplifying others' work.

The power of strategic visibility lies in its steadiness. Unlike bursts of self-promotion that quickly fade, a quiet but consistent presence builds trust over time. When people repeatedly see your name associated with thoughtful contributions, they begin to associate that name with credibility. You don't need to be everywhere, and you don't need to dominate conversations. You just need to be present where it matters most.

Many people hesitate to become more visible because they fear seeming arrogant. But strategic visibility isn't about ego; it's about clarity. It's about ensuring that your work, your ideas, and your contributions are not hidden in the background. The people who get opportunities aren't always the most talented—they're often the ones who are simply *seen*. If you do good work but no one knows about it, it remains invisible. Visibility ensures your work reaches the people who can value it.

The art is to do this without falling into the trap of constant self-promotion. One of the most effective ways to achieve this is by making your presence useful to others. Sharing a resource, offering insight on a challenge, recommending someone else, asking thoughtful questions—these actions highlight your engagement without making the moment about you. Ironically, the less you talk about yourself directly, the more memorable your presence becomes.

Another aspect of visibility is timing. Not every moment is the right moment to speak up. Visibility built on noise can fade as quickly as it appears. But visibility built on relevance endures. When you speak at the right time, when you share something meaningful, when your contributions elevate the conversation rather than distract from it, people take notice.

It's also essential to align your visibility with your values. Not every platform, event, or space deserves your energy. Being visible everywhere is not only unsustainable but also ineffective. Choose the spaces that resonate with your goals, your interests, and your professional identity. When your presence is aligned with your purpose, it feels less like effort and more like a natural extension of who you are.

Another subtle but powerful part of strategic visibility is consistency. One thoughtful interaction is easily forgotten. But repeated, meaningful contributions create a pattern. People start to recognize your voice, your perspective, your presence. You don't need to manufacture a persona to achieve this. Your authentic engagement, over time, will shape how people perceive you.

Visibility is also reinforced through storytelling. That doesn't mean broadcasting every detail of your career. It means finding ways to frame your experiences, your insights, or your learnings in a way that others can relate to. When people understand *why* you care about what you do, they connect with you more deeply. That connection makes your presence stick.

Crucially, visibility should never feel like a performance. The more you try to control how others perceive you, the more distant and artificial you become. But when your visibility is the natural byproduct of showing up authentically, your reputation grows quietly and powerfully.

For example, imagine two professionals at a networking event. One spends the entire evening talking about their achievements, their goals, their skills. The other listens intently, asks thoughtful questions, and contributes one or two meaningful insights. When people leave that event, they may not remember every detail of the second person's background, but they will remember how that person made them feel. And that memory is far more powerful than any sales pitch.

The same applies online. Someone who relentlessly promotes themselves may gain temporary attention but rarely earns trust. Someone who consistently adds value—without shouting—builds a reputation that lasts.

Strategic visibility also requires letting go of the fear of being overlooked. Many people remain silent in professional spaces because they fear judgment. But silence rarely builds recognition. You don't need to be perfect to be visible. You need to be present. Even imperfect contributions, when made with sincerity, carry more weight than perfect silence.

Over time, this quiet visibility weaves a powerful network around you. People begin to associate your name with value, presence, and credibility. You stop feeling like you have to chase every opportunity because opportunities begin to find you.

True networking isn't about pushing yourself into the spotlight. It's about showing up with substance, letting your presence speak for itself, and allowing trust to grow organically. That kind of visibility doesn't scream—but it echoes. It lingers. And most importantly, it builds a reputation that opens doors long after a single conversation has ended.

Chapter 5: Preparing for the Interview with Confidence and Clarity

5.1 Shifting Your Mindset: From Evaluation to Conversation

Interviews are often imagined as high-stakes auditions—moments where the candidate stands under a bright, metaphorical spotlight, being judged for their worth. This perception is what makes interviews feel intimidating, even for highly qualified individuals. It's what makes your heart race before you enter the room or join the video call. But this view of the interview process is deeply incomplete. It reduces the encounter to a one-way evaluation, when in reality, a strong interview is a two-way conversation.

Shifting your mindset from "I'm being tested" to "We're exploring whether this is a good fit" changes everything. It doesn't remove the pressure entirely, but it reframes it. It turns a rigid, stressful interaction into a dynamic exchange between two parties who are both evaluating whether they want to work together. This is a crucial mental shift, because confidence in interviews doesn't come only from memorizing answers or rehearsing scripts. It comes from understanding your own value and approaching the conversation as an equal participant rather than a desperate applicant.

When candidates walk into an interview seeing themselves as the ones being judged, they often unconsciously give away their power. They overcompensate, speak too quickly, undersell their experience, or contort their answers to fit what they imagine the interviewer wants to hear. They forget that interviews are not courts of judgment—they are professional dialogues. The employer wants to know whether you have the skills, the mindset, and the personality to contribute meaningfully. But equally, you should want to know whether this organization, team, and role align with the life and work you want to build.

This doesn't mean arrogance. It means balance. It means walking into the room understanding that your time, energy, and skills have value. The employer has a need; you bring potential solutions to that need. That's the real dynamic—not a power imbalance, but a mutual exploration.

To fully internalize this shift, it helps to understand what's happening on the other side of the table. Interviewers are not looking for perfection. They're looking for clarity, confidence, and fit. They want to see how your story aligns with their needs. They want to understand whether they can trust you with responsibility, whether they can imagine working alongside you, whether you'll thrive in their environment. They're evaluating your answers, yes—but they're also picking up on your energy, your presence, your ability to listen and think.

Most interviewers, whether they say it or not, are hoping the candidate in front of them will be the right one. They're rooting for you to do well. Why? Because hiring is hard, expensive, and time-consuming. No one wants to sit through endless rounds of interviews. If you can demonstrate alignment clearly and confidently, you're not an inconvenience—you're a solution to their problem.

Once you understand this, the interview stops being a performance and starts being a conversation between two people who both have something at stake. This mindset alone can dissolve a significant portion of the fear surrounding interviews. Instead of trying to "prove" yourself, you're there to explore whether there's a mutual match.

Confidence in interviews also stems from grounding yourself in your own story. If you've taken the time to clarify your purpose, understand your strengths, and shape your narrative—as outlined in earlier chapters—you already have the foundation for strong, authentic answers. The interview isn't the moment to reinvent your story; it's the moment to share it with calm conviction. When you know why you're there and what you bring, the conversation becomes less about performing and more about articulating truth.

Many people mistakenly think confidence is about being flawless. They imagine that the best candidates are the ones who never hesitate, never stumble, and always deliver perfectly polished answers. But real confidence isn't about perfection—it's about presence. Interviewers are far more impressed by a candidate who speaks with thoughtful clarity than by one who rattles off memorized lines. A moment of pausing to think is not a weakness; it's often a sign of maturity.

Approaching an interview as a conversation also allows you to be more curious. Too often, candidates forget that they are also interviewing the company. They focus so much on trying to be liked that they forget to ask themselves whether they like what they see. When you allow yourself to ask meaningful questions, when you show genuine interest in understanding how the organization works, you demonstrate not just preparedness, but discernment.

This is not only good strategy; it's good psychology. Curiosity shifts your focus outward, away from your own nerves. It keeps the interaction dynamic. When you listen actively and respond thoughtfully, the interview stops being a rigid Q&A and becomes a dialogue—an exchange between professionals. That kind of energy is memorable. It makes you stand out not through performance, but through genuine engagement.

Of course, interviews still carry stakes. You want the job. You want to make a good impression. Pretending otherwise doesn't help. But acknowledging that truth without letting it control you is the key. When your entire sense of worth is tied to the outcome of a single interview, every question becomes a test, every pause a potential failure. But when you view the interview as one step in a larger journey—a mutual exploration rather than a judgment—you give yourself the freedom to show up more fully.

It's also worth recognizing that interviewers are human beings, not gatekeeping machines. They bring their own anxieties, expectations, and biases into the room. Sometimes their questions won't be perfectly phrased. Sometimes they'll be distracted. Sometimes they'll be just as nervous as you are, especially if they're new to hiring. Remembering their humanity helps you stop over-interpreting every micro-expression and tone shift. It allows you to focus on the conversation rather than on reading imagined signals.

A conversation-based mindset also protects your confidence in the face of challenging questions. When you expect an interview to be an exam, a tough or unexpected question can feel like failure. But when you view it as a dialogue, those questions become opportunities to think, engage, and demonstrate adaptability. You don't need to have every answer memorized. What matters is how you respond, how you think out loud, how you maintain composure.

Some of the most powerful interviews happen when both sides feel free to be honest. If a question stumps you, acknowledging it and talking through your thought process is often more impactful than delivering a forced or rehearsed response. This honesty builds trust, and trust is often more influential in hiring decisions than a perfect answer.

A major part of this mindset shift involves detaching your self-worth from the outcome of the interview. Getting a "no" doesn't mean you're not capable. It often means the fit wasn't right. Organizations look for alignment across many dimensions—experience, skills, values, timing, team dynamics. Many of these factors are outside your control. Viewing the process through this lens allows you to stay grounded. Rejections become data, not personal verdicts.

It's also essential to enter an interview with clarity about your own non-negotiables. When you're desperate for an offer, any company can start to look like the right one. But if you've done the work to understand your values, your vision, and your goals, you can evaluate opportunities with discernment. This turns interviews into mutual vetting processes rather than one-sided trials.

One subtle but profound result of this mindset shift is the way it affects your body language and voice. When you believe you're there to prove yourself, your gestures may shrink, your voice may tighten, your energy may waver. But when you see yourself as an equal participant, your presence expands naturally. You sit more upright, your breathing steadies, your tone becomes warmer and more grounded. Interviewers pick up on these cues unconsciously.

Reframing interviews in this way doesn't mean you'll stop being nervous. Nerves are natural. They signal that something matters to you. But nerves become manageable when they're not amplified by a sense of powerlessness. When you step into an interview with the understanding that you're not just being evaluated—you're also evaluating—the dynamic shifts.

This mindset also has long-term benefits beyond a single job application. Over time, you stop approaching interviews as rare, high-stakes performances and start seeing them as part of an ongoing professional dialogue. Each conversation—whether it leads to an offer or not—becomes an opportunity to sharpen your narrative, refine your understanding of what you want, and expand your network.

The truth is, interviews are rarely about who can deliver the most rehearsed answers. They're about who can create a sense of clarity, trust, and alignment. When you walk in as an equal, when you focus on connection rather than fear, when you see the interviewer not as a gatekeeper but as a potential future collaborator, you transform the entire experience.

Confidence is not about erasing uncertainty. It's about standing firmly in your value while embracing the unknown. And that is exactly the energy that makes interviews not just bearable, but powerful. It's what turns a nerve-wracking encounter into an open door. It's what allows you to walk out of the room, regardless of the outcome, knowing that you showed up fully—not as a performance, but as yourself.

5.2 Understanding What Interviewers Are Really Looking For

One of the most powerful ways to walk into an interview with confidence is to understand what's happening on the other side of the table. Candidates often focus so intently on preparing answers that they forget the interview is not simply a test of their abilities. It's a structured conversation with a specific purpose for the employer: to determine whether this person—not just their résumé, but their presence, attitude, and potential—fits the role and the team.

Understanding this perspective shifts your approach. Instead of trying to guess the "right" answers, you begin to align your responses with what the interviewer is actually seeking. And what they are seeking is rarely perfection. It is clarity, consistency, and a sense that you will contribute positively to their environment.

When an interviewer evaluates you, they are not just listening to your words. They are assessing patterns. They're trying to understand what kind of colleague you would be. How you think. How you react under pressure. How you communicate. Whether your skills match their immediate needs and whether your personality and values align with their culture. Many candidates misunderstand this, believing that an interview is purely about technical competence or a flawless professional history. In reality, it's also about trust. Can they trust you to handle the responsibilities of the role? Can they trust you to collaborate well with others? Can they trust you to grow with the company?

Interviewers also want to understand your motivation. They are asking themselves, often silently, why you want to be here. Do you actually understand their mission, their challenges, their values? Are you applying because this job is genuinely a meaningful next step for you, or are you simply sending out applications indiscriminately? This distinction matters. A candidate who shows a clear, well-grounded sense of purpose is far more memorable than someone who can list skills without a coherent narrative.

This is why preparation isn't just about rehearsing answers. It's about internalizing your story. If you can articulate why this role aligns with your experience, strengths, and values, you relieve the interviewer of the burden of connecting those dots themselves. You make their job easier. You guide their perception of you, rather than leaving it to chance.

Another crucial element interviewers are evaluating is how you handle ambiguity. Interviews, almost by design, involve questions that don't have perfect answers. Sometimes they'll throw you a scenario that doesn't have a single correct solution just to see how you think. They're less interested in whether you solve it flawlessly and more interested in your reasoning process. Do you approach the problem logically? Do you remain composed when faced with uncertainty? Do you ask clarifying questions or freeze up when something unexpected arises?

Interviewers also pay close attention to the energy you bring. This is often intangible, but it matters immensely. It's not about forced enthusiasm or artificial cheerfulness; it's about demonstrating genuine interest and engagement. When someone speaks with a grounded, calm energy and clear purpose, it reassures the interviewer. It tells them: "This person understands what they want. This person is someone I could see working with every day."

Communication style is another silent but powerful dimension. You may have all the qualifications in the world, but if your communication is scattered, overly rehearsed, or evasive, it creates friction. Interviewers want to see that you can express your thoughts clearly and that you can listen as well as speak. Good interviews aren't one-way performances—they're conversations where both sides are attentive.

Cultural fit and team dynamics play an even larger role than most candidates realize. Skills can be taught, but personality alignment and attitude often determine long-term success. Interviewers are trying to imagine you as part of their existing structure. They're asking themselves: Will this person collaborate well with others? Will they add positive energy to the team, or disrupt it? Do they share or at least respect the values that define how we work?

That's why it's so important not to try to mimic what you think they want to hear. If you pretend to be someone you're not just to secure an offer, it might work in the short term, but it often leads to misalignment and dissatisfaction down the line. Authenticity allows both parties to see clearly whether the fit is real. If it isn't, walking away is not failure—it's wisdom.

Interviewers are also sensitive to confidence, though not in the loud, performative way people sometimes imagine. What impresses them is quiet assurance—the kind that comes from knowing your value, not from trying to prove it. They can tell when someone is comfortable in their own professional skin. They can also sense when someone is hiding behind memorized lines. Confidence in this context means being able to speak about your experience naturally, to acknowledge what you know and what you don't, to demonstrate curiosity and humility without undermining your competence.

They are also watching how you respond to pressure. This doesn't mean they're trying to trick or humiliate you. It means they want to see whether you can stay centered. Even small moments—how you respond when a question surprises you, how you handle a pause, how you navigate an unfamiliar scenario—give them insight into how you might behave in the real workplace.

Equally important is how you engage with their questions. Do you actually listen and respond thoughtfully, or do you rush to deliver pre-packaged answers? Are you present in the moment, or lost in the performance of what you think they want? Genuine listening and grounded responses signal maturity. They tell the interviewer they're not dealing with someone desperate to please but with a thoughtful professional who can hold their own.

Another unspoken thing interviewers look for is alignment with the company's trajectory. Even if the job is immediate, they're often thinking long term. Is this someone who will grow with us? Does this person seem adaptable? Will they contribute not just to their role but to the company's evolving goals? That doesn't mean you need to promise to stay for decades. It means you should be able to show that your interests and the company's direction intersect meaningfully.

Finally, they're observing how well you connect with them on a human level. People often underestimate the role of personal chemistry in hiring decisions. You can have two equally qualified candidates, but the one who creates a sense of rapport—who makes the conversation feel real rather than stiff—often leaves a stronger impression. This isn't about forcing charm. It's about being present, curious, and respectful.

When you understand what interviewers are really looking for, preparation becomes more focused and less overwhelming. You no longer need to prepare for every possible question like a scripted performance. Instead, you prepare to bring your story to life clearly and confidently. You prepare to engage, not to perform.

And perhaps most importantly, you stop seeing the interviewer as an intimidating judge. You start seeing them for what they are: another human being trying to make a good decision. That alone can strip away a layer of fear and allow you to show up as yourself—because that is ultimately what they're trying to see.

5.3 Preparing Strategically, Not Mechanically

Once you understand what interviewers are really looking for, your preparation takes on a different shape. Instead of trying to memorize perfect answers, you prepare strategically. Strategic preparation is about building familiarity with your own story, anticipating the flow of a conversation, and creating enough internal clarity that you can adapt to any question naturally.

Many candidates approach preparation mechanically. They look up lists of "top 50 interview questions," memorize scripted responses, and hope they can deliver them flawlessly. The problem with this approach is that real interviews are never identical to those lists. They're fluid, unpredictable, and shaped by the interviewer's personality, the company's culture, and the rhythm of the conversation. A rigid script can crack the moment something unexpected happens.

Strategic preparation, on the other hand, is less about memorization and more about grounding. It's about deeply knowing your experiences, your achievements, your values, and your goals. When you understand your story from the inside out, you don't need to cling to memorized lines. You can speak with ease because what you're saying is real.

This kind of preparation begins with clarity. Reflect on the core moments of your professional journey—the experiences that have shaped your skills and your identity. Know why they matter. Know how they connect to the role you're pursuing. When you can tell your story with that level of clarity, you can adapt it to different kinds of questions without losing coherence.

Another element of strategic preparation is familiarity with the company. Interviewers notice when a candidate has taken the time to understand their world. That doesn't mean memorizing their website word for word. It means having a real sense of what they do, how they position themselves, and why this role matters in that context. When you understand their challenges and ambitions, your answers naturally feel more relevant.

A strategic candidate also prepares mentally, not just verbally. This means rehearsing how to stay calm under pressure, how to handle silence without panicking, how to redirect your thoughts when a question surprises you. Interviews are unpredictable by nature, but when you've built your internal foundation, unpredictability becomes manageable.

Another overlooked aspect of strategic preparation is learning to speak like a human, not a résumé. Many people over-rehearse their answers until they sound like they're reading a script. This not only feels artificial but also makes it harder to connect. When your preparation is rooted in genuine understanding rather than memorization, your answers become more fluid, conversational, and believable.

Confidence also grows from practice—not the kind of robotic repetition that dulls your voice, but the kind that helps your story settle into your bones. Practicing aloud with a trusted friend or in front of a mirror can reveal where your phrasing feels forced and where your natural voice comes through. The goal isn't to sound perfect. It's to sound grounded.

Strategic preparation also means knowing your boundaries and priorities. Interviews are as much about you choosing them as them choosing you. If you're clear on your values, your goals, and your deal breakers, you'll approach the conversation with more ease. You'll be able to ask better questions, evaluate their answers, and sense whether the fit is right. This gives you a subtle but powerful confidence: you're not just hoping to be chosen, you're choosing too.

It's also worth preparing for the emotional dimension of interviews. Nerves are natural. They don't make you weak; they make you human. The goal is not to eliminate them but to work with them. Breathing exercises, grounding techniques, or even a quiet moment to center yourself before the interview can make a significant difference. Confidence isn't the absence of anxiety—it's the ability to carry it without letting it control you.

Strategic preparation also involves anticipating common types of questions—not to memorize answers, but to understand the logic behind them. When an interviewer asks about a past challenge, they're not testing your memory. They want to see how you approach problems. When they ask why you want the job, they want to understand your motivation. When they ask where you see yourself in five years, they're testing alignment. Understanding the *why* behind questions makes it easier to respond authentically.

Another subtle aspect of preparation is learning how to handle imperfection. No interview goes perfectly. There will always be a question that catches you off guard, a moment where you pause longer than expected, or an answer you wish you'd phrased differently. Strategic preparation doesn't protect you from these moments—it teaches you how to recover from them gracefully.

This ability to recover is often what interviewers remember most. A candidate who stumbles but regains composure with honesty and poise often leaves a stronger impression than someone who tries to fake their way through. It shows resilience, self-awareness, and maturity.

Preparation is also about energy management. If you've spent hours memorizing answers the night before, you may walk into the interview exhausted and tense. But if your preparation has been steady, clear, and paced over time, you'll arrive centered. Energy speaks louder than perfect sentences.

Finally, strategic preparation builds something deeper than knowledge. It builds presence. When you know your story, when you've grounded yourself in your strengths and purpose, when you've familiarized yourself with the company and the flow of interviews, you walk in with a kind of quiet confidence that doesn't need to be performed. It simply radiates.

This is the difference between someone who is trying to pass a test and someone who is ready to have a meaningful conversation. And interviews, when stripped of the fear and performance, are exactly that: conversations between two parties deciding whether to walk the same path. Strategic preparation gives you the clarity to show up fully in that moment—not as a scripted version of yourself, but as the person you actually are. And that is exactly who they need to meet.

Chapter 6: Navigating the Interview with Presence and Poise

6.1 Owning the Room (or the Screen): The Power of First Moments

An interview begins long before the first question is asked. In fact, it starts the moment you enter the space—or, in today's world, the moment your camera turns on. First moments carry weight. They shape perceptions, often in ways neither party is fully aware of. Long before you've shared your achievements or explained your qualifications, the interviewer has formed an impression of you. This impression isn't based on your answers but on the way you *arrive*.

Owning the room—or the screen—is not about dominating it. It's not about trying to be the most charismatic person they've ever met. It's about walking into the space with calm, grounded energy that communicates one simple message: "I belong here." That sense of belonging is not arrogance. It's quiet confidence. It tells the interviewer that you value your presence as much as theirs, that you see this as a conversation between equals.

First impressions aren't created through elaborate performances. They're formed through small, subtle signals: your posture, your breathing, your eye contact, your tone of voice, the pace of your movements. They emerge from how you inhabit your own body. Nervous energy shows in scattered gestures, rushed speech, fidgeting, or avoiding eye contact. Grounded energy shows in stillness, deliberate movement, and attentive presence. The goal isn't to fake confidence but to access it.

A strong entrance begins with awareness. Take a moment before the interview to center yourself—not by repeating artificial affirmations, but by grounding your attention in the present moment. Whether you're walking into a physical room or logging onto a video call, that short transition is powerful. It's a breath between your preparation and your performance, between your expectations and reality. A single calm breath can reset your entire nervous system.

The way you greet the interviewer matters more than most people realize. A greeting isn't just a formality. It sets the tone for the entire conversation. A rushed "hello" mumbled while adjusting your seat creates a different atmosphere than a clear, warm "hello" delivered with steady eye contact and a composed presence. This doesn't mean overdoing friendliness or performing enthusiasm. It means acknowledging that those first seconds are your opportunity to set the emotional temperature of the room.

The energy you project at the beginning influences not only how they perceive you but also how you perceive yourself. If you approach the moment as a test, your body reacts with tension. If you approach it as a conversation with a peer, your body loosens. Your breathing steadies. Your voice deepens. People sense that shift instinctively. Interviewers are not consciously dissecting your posture or tone, but they *feel* the difference between someone who is grounded and someone who is grasping for approval.

This principle applies equally to in-person and virtual interviews, though the mediums differ. In-person, your presence fills the room. Your walk, your handshake, your posture as you sit—all of these elements communicate volumes before you speak a single word. Online, the cues are subtler but no less powerful. Your camera framing, the way you look into the lens, your facial expressions, your lighting, your ability to stay present rather than distracted—all of these shape how your presence is felt through the screen.

Many candidates underestimate how much presence can be conveyed virtually. They assume a digital interview limits their ability to connect. But energy travels even through screens. A candidate who sits with an upright but relaxed posture, who listens without glancing constantly at their own image, who speaks with steady pace and warmth, creates an immediate impression of confidence. A candidate who slouches, mumbles, or lets their gaze drift looks disconnected—even if their answers are perfect.

The difference between forced confidence and real presence is subtle but undeniable. Forced confidence tries to impress. Real presence simply *is*. It doesn't try to prove worthiness because it already knows it. That doesn't mean you won't feel nervous—almost everyone does. It means you learn to hold that nervousness instead of letting it control you. You breathe into it. You stay anchored in the conversation rather than in the storm of your own thoughts.

Another overlooked part of first impressions is timing. Arriving late, even by a minute, sends an unintended message about your reliability and respect for the process. Arriving too early can also create awkwardness. But arriving on time, prepared and composed, signals readiness. In virtual interviews, this means checking your technology ahead of time—your audio, camera, background, and internet connection—so that the beginning is smooth rather than chaotic. The way the first thirty seconds unfold shapes how the rest of the conversation feels.

Your attire, though seemingly superficial, is also part of your first impression. It's not about dressing to impress in the conventional sense—it's about dressing in a way that reflects respect for the occasion and comfort in your own skin. Overdressing can make you look stiff or disconnected from the company culture; underdressing can signal carelessness. The sweet spot is attire that matches the tone of the organization while allowing you to move and breathe comfortably. If you feel physically uneasy in what you're wearing, that discomfort will leak into your presence.

But perhaps the most powerful element of a strong first impression is your internal posture—how you see yourself as you walk into that space. If you enter thinking, *I hope they like me,* your energy will be deferential, hesitant, or overly accommodating. If you enter thinking, *This is a mutual conversation,* your energy shifts. You speak more slowly. You listen more deeply. You inhabit your words instead of rushing through them.

This inner posture affects your tone of voice as well. When people are nervous or trying to impress, they often speak too quickly or pitch their voices higher without realizing it. But when they feel grounded, their voice slows and deepens slightly. It carries more weight—not because they've learned some technique, but because their mind is anchored in the moment rather than racing ahead.

Interviewers are not just listening to what you say. They're responding to how you make them feel. If your energy feels chaotic, they may find it difficult to focus on your words. If your energy feels calm and steady, they can relax into the conversation with you. The more at ease they feel in your presence, the more likely they are to remember the interaction positively.

This doesn't mean you need to be stoic or emotionless. Warmth and presence can coexist beautifully. A relaxed smile, a natural laugh, a moment of genuine curiosity—all of these small human gestures break the stiffness of formal interviews and turn them into something more organic. People don't remember robotic perfection; they remember genuine connection.

Another key part of owning those first moments is learning how to handle the surge of adrenaline that inevitably comes when the interview begins. It's normal to feel that spike of energy. The key is not to fight it but to channel it. A deep breath before speaking, a moment of eye contact, a deliberate pace—these actions transform that nervous energy into alertness. It shifts from something that undermines you to something that supports you.

It's also worth remembering that interviews are not adversarial encounters. The person sitting across from you—or appearing on your screen—is not your opponent. They're someone hoping, perhaps even eager, to find the right fit. They want this to go well. When you remember that, the first moments stop feeling like stepping onto a stage and start feeling like opening a conversation.

This mindset shift doesn't just influence how the interviewer perceives you—it influences how you perceive yourself. When you approach the interaction as a mutual exploration, your confidence is less fragile. You're not waiting for approval; you're engaging as a peer. That is the essence of presence: a quiet, unforced sense of equality.

Presence is something people feel. They can't quite define it, but they remember it. It's the difference between someone who enters a space apologizing for their existence and someone who enters knowing they have something to offer. That doesn't mean arrogance, loudness, or forced charm. It means trust in your own worth.

The beauty of presence is that it doesn't depend on external achievements. You don't need to be the most decorated candidate to own the first moments of an interview. What matters is how fully you inhabit yourself when you arrive. A candidate with modest credentials but strong presence can often outshine someone with an impressive résumé but scattered energy.

This is why those opening seconds matter so much. They don't determine everything, but they set the tone. If the interviewer feels at ease with you from the start, the entire conversation flows more naturally. If you begin rushed, disoriented, or visibly nervous, it creates a subtle barrier that you'll spend the rest of the interview trying to dismantle.

Owning the room or the screen isn't about perfection. It's about intention. It's about arriving as someone who understands their worth, who respects the space they're entering, and who is ready to engage as an equal. When you bring that kind of presence into the first moments, the rest of the interview stops feeling like a battle and starts feeling like what it truly is: a human conversation with real potential.

And in the end, that is what interviewers remember most—not just the polished sentences, but how you made them feel the moment you walked in.

6.2 Communicating with Impact and Authenticity

Once the first impression has been made, the conversation truly begins. It's here, in the flow of questions and answers, that interviews are often won or lost—not because of rigid formulas or rehearsed lines, but because of how clearly, calmly, and genuinely a candidate can communicate. Communication during an interview isn't just about what you say. It's about how you say it, how it lands in the space between you and the interviewer, and how it reflects the way you carry yourself as a professional.

Many people enter interviews believing that the key to success lies in saying something impressive at every turn. They overload their answers with jargon, inflate their achievements, or speak in polished but empty phrases they think sound "professional." Ironically, this often has the opposite effect. Interviewers don't remember the person who talks the most—they remember the person who speaks with clarity and authenticity.

Authentic communication begins with intention. Every time you respond to a question, you're not just giving information—you're shaping how the interviewer experiences you. Your words reveal how you think, what you value, how you handle complexity, and whether you can collaborate effectively. This is why the best answers aren't the longest or most elaborate ones. They are the ones that feel honest, structured, and rooted in reality.

One of the most powerful things you can do in an interview is to slow down. Nervous candidates often speak too fast, trying to get everything out before they lose their train of thought. But when you rush, your words blur together, your sentences become tangled, and your message loses its weight. Taking a brief pause before you answer—just enough to breathe and gather your thoughts—changes the rhythm of the conversation. It shows the interviewer that you're deliberate, composed, and present.

It also gives you the space to ensure your answers are clear. Clarity is far more persuasive than grandiosity. A short, focused response that communicates exactly what you mean will always land better than a rambling monologue. This is especially true when describing your experience. Instead of drowning the interviewer in a chronological list of everything you did, center your answer around what mattered most. Explain the situation, your role, the impact you made, and what you learned.

Authenticity in communication also means embracing your natural voice. Too many candidates try to adopt a corporate tone that feels stiff and impersonal, as if they're performing a role rather than being themselves. But people respond to warmth, honesty, and ease. You can be professional without being robotic. When you speak in a way that reflects who you truly are, your words carry a quiet power.

This doesn't mean being overly casual or unfiltered. Authenticity isn't about saying whatever crosses your mind. It's about letting your true perspective and personality come through, while maintaining respect for the conversation. If you care about a subject, let that care show. If you've learned something meaningful from a challenge, let that story breathe. Real stories resonate more than rehearsed sound bites.

Another dimension of impactful communication is active listening. Interviews are often misunderstood as opportunities to perform. But the strongest candidates don't dominate the conversation—they listen just as much as they speak. When you truly listen, you can tailor your answers to what's being asked, rather than launching into a pre-planned monologue. This shows agility, presence, and respect.

Listening also allows you to pick up on subtle cues—tone, body language, follow-up questions—that reveal what the interviewer actually cares about. Sometimes what they're asking isn't exactly what they mean. By staying alert and curious, you can respond to the *real* question, not just the literal one.

Nonverbal communication plays a critical role as well. It's not just your words that speak. Your posture, your facial expressions, your gestures, and even the rhythm of your breathing all send signals. An upright but relaxed posture conveys confidence without arrogance. Sustained but natural eye contact builds trust. A genuine nod when listening shows engagement. These small cues shape how your words are received, often more powerfully than the words themselves.

Voice is another subtle instrument that can either enhance or weaken your communication. A rushed, high-pitched, or overly soft voice can make your answers seem uncertain, even if your content is strong. A calm, steady tone—even if quiet—conveys authority and ease. Varying your cadence and intonation slightly also keeps the listener engaged. Monotone delivery, no matter how brilliant the content, can make your answers fade into the background.

One of the most underrated communication skills in interviews is the ability to say less. Many candidates fear silence, so they keep talking long after they've made their point. But when you fill every second with words, your impact gets diluted. Well-placed pauses allow your words to land. They give the interviewer time to absorb what you've said. They also communicate self-assurance: someone who isn't afraid of silence is someone who isn't desperate to fill the space.

Authenticity also means being able to admit when you don't know something. Interviewers can tell when a candidate is trying to bluff their way through an unfamiliar question. Acknowledging the limits of your knowledge—while showing your ability to think critically or express how you'd approach learning something—often earns far more respect than a shaky, overcompensating answer.

This ability to own what you know and what you don't is a mark of maturity. It demonstrates self-awareness, which is a trait employers value deeply. Companies don't need candidates who know everything. They need people who can think clearly, communicate honestly, and grow.

Another powerful layer of communication is storytelling. Facts and figures inform; stories make people feel. When you ground your answers in real experiences—moments that reveal how you solved a problem, learned something, or grew as a professional—

you become memorable. A story well told doesn't need to be dramatic. It just needs to be clear, honest, and relevant.

Interviewers meet many candidates with similar qualifications. What sets you apart is not just what you've done, but how you make your experiences come alive. When your words paint a clear picture, they create a lasting impression.

But none of this works without presence. Communication isn't just a transfer of information; it's an exchange of energy. If your mind is racing ahead to the next question, your words will lose their weight. If you're fully in the moment, even simple answers can land with quiet authority. That's what makes a candidate unforgettable—not slickness, but sincerity.

6.3 Responding with Composure and Depth

Every interview, no matter how well prepared you are, will contain unexpected moments. There will be questions that catch you off guard, topics that feel challenging, or moments of silence that stretch longer than expected. The way you respond in these moments is often just as important—sometimes more so—than the content of your prepared answers. Responding with composure and depth is about trusting yourself enough to handle uncertainty gracefully.

The first and most important skill in these situations is to pause. Too many candidates panic the moment they hear a question they didn't anticipate. They rush to speak, fearing that silence will make them look unprepared. But silence, when used intentionally, can communicate the opposite. A brief pause to gather your thoughts signals thoughtfulness and confidence. It shows that you are not simply reacting—you are reflecting.

Composure is not the absence of nerves; it's the ability to remain steady despite them. When an interviewer asks something complex, it's natural for your mind to race. But if you can stay anchored in your breath and give yourself even a moment to think, you reclaim control of the conversation. This moment of steadiness can turn a potentially awkward question into an opportunity to demonstrate poise.

Depth in your answers doesn't mean overloading them with details. It means speaking from understanding rather than fear. Even if you don't have the perfect answer, you can demonstrate depth by showing how you think. If you're presented with a scenario, talk through your reasoning process calmly. Let them see how you approach challenges, how you organize your thoughts, and how you make decisions. That's often more valuable than a "right" answer.

This skill becomes especially important with behavioral and situational questions—those that begin with "Tell me about a time when…" or "How would you handle if…". These questions are designed not just to test your memory, but to reveal how you think and act under pressure. A shallow answer might list what happened. A deeper one reflects on why it happened, what you learned, and how it shaped your approach moving forward.

Composure also plays a critical role in how you handle emotionally charged or unexpected questions. Sometimes an interviewer will probe into a challenging period of your career, a failure, or a gap in your résumé. These are moments where defensiveness can easily creep in. But when you answer calmly, acknowledging what happened without apology or panic, you transform a potential vulnerability into a moment of strength.

Depth comes from reflection. If you've taken the time before the interview to truly understand your experiences—the wins, the setbacks, the lessons learned—you won't need to scramble for words when difficult questions arise. You'll already know how to speak about those moments with honesty and perspective.

Another key to responding with depth is avoiding the temptation to overperform. Some candidates respond to pressure by turning up the volume—speaking faster, smiling harder, or throwing in big, impressive-sounding phrases. But overcompensation often reads as insecurity. Composure, on the other hand, radiates quiet confidence. A steady pace, a measured voice, and a thoughtful tone say far more than frantic enthusiasm ever could.

Your body language also plays a significant role here. When you remain still, when your gestures are controlled and your posture open, you give the impression of someone who is at ease with themselves. That impression can be powerful even if you're improvising your answer in the moment. Conversely, fidgeting, avoiding eye contact, or collapsing your posture can undermine even the strongest response.

Depth is also about connection. When you respond thoughtfully, you invite the interviewer into your thinking. You make the conversation collaborative rather than defensive. This is particularly effective when the interviewer asks something provocative or challenging. Instead of seeing the question as an attack, see it as an invitation to engage. Ask a clarifying question if needed. Reflect out loud. Show that you're not just answering—you're engaging with the idea behind the question.

This ability to stay composed and think deeply also extends to moments when you simply don't know the answer. Everyone faces these moments. What matters is how you handle them. Admitting that you don't have an immediate answer, but showing how you would approach finding one, can be far more impressive than pretending to know. It shows humility, resourcefulness, and intellectual honesty.

Composure is equally important at the emotional level. Interviews can stir up vulnerability—especially when they touch on parts of your story that were difficult. The key is not to shut those emotions down, but to hold them with dignity. If you speak about a challenging period, let the lesson shine brighter than the struggle. When you own your story fully, even the difficult parts, it shows resilience.

Finally, responding with composure and depth means remembering that you are allowed to take space. Too often, candidates shrink themselves in interviews, as if they have to earn the right to exist in the room. But when you allow yourself to breathe, to think, to take a moment, you silently affirm your worth. You remind both yourself and the interviewer that this is a conversation between equals.

The truth is, no one expects you to be flawless. Interviewers expect you to be human. They expect moments of hesitation. What sets strong candidates apart is not their ability to avoid those moments, but their ability to navigate them with calmness and depth.

When you can do that—when you can pause, reflect, and speak from a grounded place—you turn uncertainty into strength. You transform silence into weight. You make your words land with more power because they come from a centered, thoughtful place. And long after the interview is over, that presence, that quiet steadiness, is what lingers in the interviewer's memory.

Chapter 7: Answering Questions with Strategy and Substance

7.1 Mastering Behavioral Questions

For many candidates, behavioral questions are the most daunting part of an interview. They can feel unpredictable, personal, and difficult to rehearse. Unlike technical questions that assess concrete skills, behavioral questions dig deeper. They aim to reveal how you think, how you respond to challenges, how you interact with others, and how you behave when things don't go according to plan. They give interviewers something résumés can't: a glimpse of who you are when the spotlight is off and the pressure is on.

These questions are often introduced with familiar phrases: "Tell me about a time when…," "Describe a situation where…," or "Give me an example of how you handled…." They're not just interested in the situation itself; they're interested in the story you tell about it. Your answer becomes a living example of your working style, your emotional intelligence, and your problem-solving ability.

To handle these moments with strength, you need to approach them strategically—not with a rigid script, but with clarity, structure, and self-awareness. A behavioral question is less about whether you faced an extraordinary situation and more about how clearly and thoughtfully you can articulate your response. Even a seemingly ordinary example can be compelling if it reveals something meaningful about how you operate.

The first key to mastering behavioral questions is understanding what the interviewer is truly looking for. They're not searching for a heroic tale. They want to see how you approach challenges, how you make decisions, how you work with others, and what kind of mindset you bring to your professional life. They want to see whether you take ownership of your actions and whether you can learn from experience.

When faced with these questions, many candidates make the mistake of giving vague or abstract answers. They describe what "usually happens" or what they "would do" rather than what they actually did. That approach strips the story of its power. Specificity is what makes your answers credible. Interviewers want to hear about real moments that reveal real behavior. A well-told story rooted in your own experience carries far more weight than theoretical statements.

This is why reflection before an interview matters so much. If you've already taken the time to think about meaningful moments in your professional journey—challenges you've faced, conflicts you've resolved, projects you've led, mistakes you've learned from—you won't have to scramble for examples under pressure. You'll be able to respond with calm clarity, because the story is already yours to tell.

The most compelling behavioral answers have a clear beginning, middle, and end. They set the stage with context, describe your actions in a way that highlights your agency, and close with the outcome or what you learned. But what makes them resonate is not the structure alone—it's your ownership of the narrative. It's the sense that you are not a passive character in the story, but its active driver.

Take, for example, a common behavioral question: "Tell me about a time you faced a challenge at work and how you dealt with it." A weak response might be a general statement about working well under pressure. A strong response paints a picture: the specific challenge, your reasoning as you navigated it, the actions you took, and the results that followed. Even if the outcome wasn't perfect, what matters most is how clearly you can articulate your thinking and growth.

Another common question might focus on conflict: "Tell me about a time you disagreed with a colleague or manager." Many candidates tense up when they hear this, worried that admitting to conflict will make them look difficult. But interviewers aren't looking for a flawless record. They're looking for emotional intelligence. They want to see how you handle disagreements professionally, how you balance honesty with respect, and how you work toward resolution.

This is why self-awareness is one of your greatest assets in behavioral interviews. If you can speak about your experiences honestly—acknowledging your role, your reasoning, and your growth—you signal maturity. You show that you're not threatened by difficult conversations but capable of navigating them with composure.

Another reason these questions are powerful is that they allow interviewers to test alignment between your words and your actions. Anyone can claim to be "a good communicator," "a strong leader," or "a team player." But when you describe a real situation where you demonstrated those qualities, your claims become tangible. Behavioral answers are proof, not promises.

To deliver these stories effectively, you need to be comfortable inhabiting your own experiences. Nervous candidates often rush through their answers, afraid of boring the interviewer or revealing too much. But when you slow down and tell the story with quiet confidence, it becomes more than an answer. It becomes a window into how you operate under pressure.

Another common challenge is choosing the "right" example. Many candidates assume they need to share their most dramatic or impressive story. In reality, a simple, well-articulated story often lands better than a complex, chaotic one. The goal is not to impress with scale; it's to reveal clarity in how you think and act. Even a modest example can be powerful if you frame it thoughtfully.

It's also important to maintain emotional presence when telling these stories. If you recite your answer like a memorized script, the story loses its power. But when you speak as someone revisiting a real moment—someone who lived through it and learned from it—the interviewer feels that authenticity. They can sense the reality behind the words.

Another aspect of behavioral questions that often goes overlooked is how they allow you to shape the narrative of your candidacy. Instead of waiting passively for the interviewer to uncover who you are, you can use these stories to highlight the qualities you want them to remember. Each answer is an opportunity to reinforce the image of the professional you are and the colleague you could be.

Interviewers also pay close attention to how you talk about other people in your behavioral stories. If your answers are full of blame, resentment, or distance, it signals potential problems with teamwork or accountability. But if your language reflects fairness, responsibility, and an understanding of different perspectives, it shows emotional intelligence.

Behavioral questions are also an opportunity to demonstrate adaptability. For example, if you're asked about a time when something didn't go as planned, the point is not to prove you always succeed. It's to show that you can remain steady, learn, and adjust when challenges arise. Interviewers respect candidates who can speak about failures without defensiveness. It shows resilience and growth.

Confidence in answering behavioral questions doesn't come from memorizing perfect stories. It comes from having done the inner work to understand your own path. If you've reflected on your challenges, your achievements, your turning points, and your lessons learned, you don't need to manufacture the right words. They'll flow more naturally because they're yours.

It's also important to let the story breathe. Many candidates rush through their answers, trying to "get it over with." But when you allow your story to unfold at a measured pace—without rambling or rushing—you give it weight. You give the interviewer space to imagine the situation and understand your role within it.

Interviewers don't expect flawless stories. They expect real ones. They want to see the arc of how you think, act, and grow. That's why even stories about mistakes or setbacks can be incredibly powerful when told with clarity and reflection. If you can articulate what went wrong, what you learned, and how it changed your approach, you turn a moment of imperfection into a story of strength.

Behavioral questions are not traps. They are invitations—to speak about your work, your values, your decision-making, and your resilience. When you approach them not with fear but with curiosity and confidence, they become one of the most effective ways to differentiate yourself from other candidates.

In the end, mastering behavioral questions is less about technique and more about self-knowledge. When you know your story, when you understand how your experiences have shaped you, and when you can communicate that with honesty and presence, you stop sounding like a candidate trying to impress. You sound like a professional who knows their worth. And that is what makes interviewers remember you.

7.2 Handling Difficult or Unexpected Questions with Grace

Every interview has its unpredictable moments. No matter how much you prepare, there will come a question that lands in a way you didn't anticipate. It might touch on something sensitive—like a gap in your résumé, a past failure, or a technical detail you don't know. It might be phrased vaguely or confrontationally. Or it might be one of those curveball questions designed to test how you think on your feet.

Many candidates panic at these moments. Their breathing quickens. Their mind scrambles for a "right" answer. But the truth is, difficult questions are rarely designed to trap you. More often, they're opportunities for the interviewer to understand how you handle discomfort, how you respond to ambiguity, and how you manage your own presence under pressure.

When these moments arise, your first instinct might be to fill the silence with words. But the most powerful first response is a pause. Even a two- or three-second pause can make all the difference. It allows you to collect your thoughts, slow your heartbeat, and create space for a deliberate response. Silence in an interview doesn't signal incompetence. It signals composure.

In fact, how you *handle* the pause often communicates more than what you eventually say. An anxious, frantic rush to speak can make even a good answer sound shaky. But a calm, measured breath before you respond tells the interviewer you can stay grounded when things get difficult. That quality—steadiness in the face of uncertainty—is something most organizations deeply value.

Another crucial skill in these moments is acknowledging what's happening rather than trying to cover it up. If you need a moment to think, you can say so with quiet confidence: "That's a good question. Let me take a second to think about it." This kind of statement doesn't weaken your position; it strengthens it. It shows you can regulate your own reactions, which is a mark of emotional intelligence and maturity.

When the question itself feels confusing or vague, resist the temptation to guess what they meant. Instead, ask for clarification. A simple, composed follow-up—"Could you elaborate a bit on what you mean by that?" or "Just to make sure I understand, are you asking about…"—gives you both clarity and a moment to breathe. Interviewers appreciate candidates who can engage with questions thoughtfully rather than rushing to answer blindly.

There will also be times when the question exposes an area where you lack experience or knowledge. These moments can feel threatening, but they don't have to be. Interviewers aren't expecting omniscience; they're evaluating how you respond to gaps. Trying to fake an answer is risky—not only because it can backfire, but because it erodes trust. A calm acknowledgment, combined with a proactive mindset, is far more powerful. For example, if you're unfamiliar with a particular tool, methodology, or situation, expressing how you would approach learning or solving it can turn a potential weakness into an example of adaptability.

Difficult questions also include personal ones—about mistakes, weaknesses, or failures. These are often where candidates feel the most exposed. The instinct to downplay, deflect, or mask those experiences is understandable. But interviewers usually see through evasiveness. What resonates far more is honesty paired with reflection. Admitting a past shortcoming doesn't make you weak if it's accompanied by clarity about how you learned from it and how it shaped your professional growth.

For example, if asked about a mistake, some candidates try to disguise strengths as weaknesses: "I work too hard" or "I care too much." Interviewers recognize this tactic instantly, and it can feel insincere. But a well-considered, genuine example—a real challenge, explained with self-awareness and an emphasis on growth—creates a very different impression. It shows you're capable of self-reflection, of recognizing your own blind spots, and of evolving. That's a trait far more valuable than superficial perfection.

Another kind of difficult question is the one that seems to challenge your decisions. An interviewer may ask why you left a particular job, why your career path looks non-linear, or why a specific project failed. These questions can feel confrontational, but they're rarely meant to attack. They're invitations to explain context and show how you handle scrutiny. If you can speak about those moments calmly, without defensiveness or self-justification, you demonstrate strength.

The key is to own your story. A career is never a straight line. Most professionals have gaps, pivots, missteps, and unexpected turns. The strongest candidates are those who can speak about these transitions with clarity, not shame. If you left a job, you can explain what you learned from the experience and why the next step made sense. If something didn't work out as planned, you can show what you took from it. When you own your path, even difficult moments become evidence of resilience.

Difficult questions also test your ability to stay emotionally balanced. Interviewers sometimes introduce tension not because they're unfriendly, but because they want to see how you respond

The 8-Week Plan to Get a New Job

to challenge. Do you crumble, become defensive, or lash out subtly? Or do you stay composed, engaged, and clear? The way you handle this dynamic can be just as revealing as the content of your answer.

Composure, however, doesn't mean emotional detachment. It's entirely possible to be warm, sincere, and steady at the same time. You can acknowledge a difficult topic with grace, without letting it derail your energy. That balance—staying open but not losing your footing—is what leaves a lasting impression.

Another subtle but important skill when facing tough questions is resisting the urge to over-explain. Nervous candidates often talk themselves in circles, trying to justify or soften their answers. Ironically, this usually makes them sound less confident. A clear, concise, and honest response, followed by a natural pause, communicates far more strength than a long, defensive speech.

This principle also applies to those notorious "gotcha" questions—like unexpected brainteasers or deliberately abstract scenarios. While these are less common today, some interviewers still use them to test adaptability rather than knowledge. If you encounter one, remember that the interviewer isn't looking for the "right" answer. They're observing how you think out loud. Do you panic? Do you shut down? Or do you engage with the question, break it down, and reason your way through it?

In these moments, vulnerability can be an asset, not a liability. Saying, "I haven't encountered that exact situation before, but here's how I would approach it," can be a perfectly strong answer. It demonstrates resourcefulness rather than fear.

Ultimately, handling difficult questions with grace comes down to trust—trust in your ability to think, to stay grounded, and to communicate your truth without collapsing under pressure. When you stop treating every hard question as a threat and start seeing it as a chance to reveal your composure, everything changes. You stop overreacting. You start listening more deeply. You let your answers breathe.

Interviewers remember these moments. They remember the candidate who stayed poised when the conversation took an unexpected turn. They remember the sense of quiet steadiness that comes from someone who trusts themselves.

This doesn't mean you have to be flawless. It means you allow yourself to be human, to acknowledge what you know and what you don't, to embrace imperfection with dignity. That's what grace looks like in an interview setting—not polished performance, but grounded presence.

7.3 Balancing Honesty and Professionalism

Among the most delicate skills in answering interview questions is the ability to tell the truth without oversharing, to be transparent without unraveling your boundaries, and to speak with sincerity without losing professionalism. This balance between honesty and composure is what often separates a good candidate from a memorable one.

Many people approach interviews as performances. They feel pressured to present a version of themselves that's polished to the point of being unrecognizable—a figure without doubts, flaws, or complicated experiences. But this is not what most interviewers actually want. They don't expect perfection. They expect clarity, maturity, and the ability to be real while respecting the professional context.

Honesty in an interview doesn't mean laying your entire personal history on the table. It means being willing to own your story. It means not hiding behind generic phrases, not disguising weaknesses as strengths, and not avoiding difficult truths out of fear. When you speak honestly—measured, clear, and without defensiveness—you build trust. And trust is one of the most powerful currencies in a hiring decision.

Professionalism, on the other hand, is the container that gives that honesty shape. It's what prevents transparency from turning into oversharing. It's what allows you to speak about setbacks, disagreements, or personal challenges without letting the conversation slip into emotional chaos. Professionalism isn't about being cold. It's about communicating with poise.

For example, consider the difference between someone explaining why they left a job with bitterness versus someone who speaks with calm clarity. The first may dwell on grievances, point fingers, or share unnecessary details. The second acknowledges the facts, frames the decision in a way that reveals learning or growth, and moves forward. Both may be telling the truth, but only one does so in a way that builds credibility.

Balancing honesty and professionalism is especially important when discussing negative experiences—such as workplace conflicts, failures, or gaps in employment. The key is to anchor your response in what you learned, not in what went wrong. When you focus on growth, you show that you can handle challenges without becoming consumed by them.

It also helps to remember that honesty doesn't require justification. If you made a decision—such as leaving a job, changing industries, or taking time off—you don't need to over-explain or apologize for it. You can state the truth clearly and calmly, then guide the conversation back to the present and your strengths. Over-apologizing or over-rationalizing can unintentionally signal insecurity.

This is why preparation matters. If you've thought carefully about how to talk about the less polished parts of your professional journey before the interview, you'll be less likely to stumble into oversharing in the moment. You'll be able to frame those experiences in a way that is honest but anchored in reflection.

There's also a subtle but powerful emotional layer to this balance. Candidates who speak with quiet honesty tend to project more confidence than those who try too hard to control how they're perceived. When you stop trying to sound "perfect," your tone relaxes. Your sentences become clearer. You communicate as a peer rather than as someone begging for approval.

Of course, honesty doesn't mean ignoring diplomacy. If you had a difficult manager or a toxic workplace, this isn't the moment to unload. Speaking negatively about former colleagues or employers rarely reflects well on a candidate, even if the story is true. The more powerful approach is to acknowledge the situation with neutrality, emphasize what you learned, and redirect the focus to what you're seeking now.

For example, instead of saying, "My manager was terrible, and the environment was toxic," you might say, "The environment wasn't the right fit for me, and it taught me a lot about the kind of culture where I thrive." This statement is still honest, but it carries professionalism, maturity, and self-awareness.

Balancing honesty and professionalism also means understanding your boundaries. There are questions that delve into sensitive personal matters—family, health, or topics that may not even be legally appropriate in some countries. You are not obligated to disclose more than you're comfortable with. If a question feels intrusive, you can respond in a way that acknowledges the topic without going into personal detail, or gently steer the conversation back to relevant professional ground.

Another crucial aspect of this balance is emotional regulation. Even when recounting challenging experiences, your tone matters as much as your words. If your voice carries bitterness, resentment, or apology, it colors how your message is received. But if your tone is measured and reflective, even a difficult story can leave a strong impression.

Interviewers often sense when a candidate is being guarded or rehearsed. They also sense when someone is trying to manipulate their perception. Neither inspires trust. But when someone speaks simply and clearly, without performance or evasion, it feels real. And realness is memorable.

This doesn't mean you need to share every detail of your professional past. In fact, part of professionalism is discernment—knowing what to share, how to share it, and when to stop. Short, clear, honest answers are often the most powerful. They communicate confidence because they don't try to overcompensate.

There is also strength in acknowledging uncertainty when it's genuine. If you don't know something, pretending you do is rarely convincing. Admitting it calmly, and showing how you would approach finding the answer, often builds more trust than a forced display of competence. Employers value adaptability and honesty far more than feigned perfection.

Ultimately, balancing honesty and professionalism is about self-respect. It's about recognizing that your story, including its imperfect parts, has value. You're not auditioning for a role in which only the most polished parts of your experience are allowed to exist. You're presenting yourself as a whole human being who can speak clearly, own their path, and stand in their truth with composure.

When you strike that balance, something subtle but powerful happens in the room. The conversation stops feeling like an interrogation and starts feeling like a genuine dialogue between adults. Interviewers lean in, not because they're dazzled by rehearsed lines, but because they trust what they're hearing.

In the end, interviews are not about projecting a flawless image. They're about building connection and trust. When honesty is paired with maturity, when vulnerability is wrapped in steadiness, you leave an impression that lasts far beyond the final handshake or the end of the video call. That impression is not built on perfection. It's built on truth spoken with dignity.

Chapter 8: Asking Questions That Build Connection and Insight

8.1 The Power of Thoughtful Questions

One of the most overlooked parts of an interview is the moment when the interviewer turns to the candidate and says, "Do you have any questions for us?" Many candidates, already exhausted by the pressure of answering, treat this as a polite formality or a test to survive. Some say "No, I think we've covered everything," eager to end the conversation. Others ask something generic and forgettable, like "What's a typical day like?" or "When will I hear back?" But in truth, this moment is one of the most powerful opportunities you have—not just to stand out, but to create a real conversation, a moment where the dynamic subtly shifts.

The questions you ask reveal far more than curiosity. They reveal how you think, what you value, and whether you approach opportunities with depth or passivity. They show whether you're someone who just wants a job, or someone who's genuinely invested in finding the right place to grow. Employers notice this distinction immediately. Candidates who ask thoughtful, well-grounded questions linger in their minds long after the conversation ends.

When you ask questions with intention, you change the energy of the interview. Up to this point, the interviewer has been in control, evaluating your fit, leading the conversation. But when it's your turn to ask questions, the power dynamic subtly levels out. You move from being evaluated to being an active participant in the decision. You signal that you are not just waiting to be chosen—you are choosing too.

This is why asking no questions, or asking shallow ones, can unintentionally weaken an otherwise strong interview. It can suggest disinterest, a lack of preparation, or a passive mindset. By contrast, thoughtful questions demonstrate engagement, critical thinking, and confidence. They say, without you needing to declare it outright: "I take this seriously. I'm discerning. I want to understand whether this is truly the right fit for both of us."

To understand the true power of thoughtful questions, it helps to shift your perspective. Interviews are not just about proving that you can do the job. They're also about determining whether the company, the team, and the environment align with your goals, values, and well-being. Asking good questions isn't just a strategy to impress; it's also a way to protect yourself from stepping into a role that doesn't support your growth.

When you ask meaningful questions, you create space for insight. You learn about the team's dynamics, the organization's priorities, the leadership's vision, and the realities of the role beyond the job description. These are details that no career website or listing can fully communicate. They're the human heartbeat of a workplace, and they can only be revealed through real conversation.

But this isn't only about gathering information—it's about the impression you leave. When you ask a question that's genuinely thoughtful, it tells the interviewer that you have the capacity to look beneath the surface. It signals emotional intelligence, initiative, and strategic thinking. It shows that you understand the professional relationship as a two-way street.

This moment also allows you to demonstrate active listening. If you've paid close attention throughout the interview, you can shape your questions in response to what the interviewer has said. Instead of pulling a rehearsed question from memory, you can build on the conversation: "Earlier, you mentioned X. I'd love to know more about how that plays out day to day." This kind of question isn't just thoughtful—it shows presence. It shows that you were not merely waiting for your turn to speak, but fully engaged in the exchange.

The tone in which you ask your questions matters as much as the content. Thoughtful questions are not interrogations. They're invitations. They're opportunities to deepen the conversation rather than put the interviewer on the defensive. When asked with genuine curiosity rather than a rehearsed or confrontational tone, they build rapport. They transform the final part of the interview from a closing formality into a meaningful exchange.

It's also important to recognize that the questions you ask tell the interviewer something about your priorities. If all your questions revolve around salary, perks, or vacation time, it can give the impression that your interest is transactional. Those topics are valid and important, but they should ideally be framed within a broader curiosity about the company's culture, values, and vision. Employers want to see that you care not just about what you'll get, but about where you're going.

Good questions also allow you to assess whether the company is the kind of place where you can truly thrive. A job that looks appealing on paper can reveal its deeper realities through how leaders and team members talk about their work. When you ask questions about how decisions are made, how teams collaborate, or how success is defined, you learn what the organization values—and whether those values align with your own.

There is a quiet confidence in asking strong questions. Candidates who approach this moment with genuine curiosity and composure often leave a deeper impression than those who rely solely on polished answers earlier in the interview. This is because strong questions suggest a level of self-assuredness: you know your worth, and you are evaluating them as much as they are evaluating you.

This moment can also be a space to build human connection. Interviews can feel formal and distant, but thoughtful questions can shift the tone toward something more personal and real. When you ask about the interviewer's own experience—why they joined the company, what they enjoy most, what challenges they've encountered—you create a conversation rather than a checklist. People remember how they felt in your presence. If the last impression they have of you is one of genuine engagement, that can carry more weight than a perfectly worded résumé.

Another often-missed aspect of asking questions is how it subtly showcases your communication style. The way you phrase a question reveals how you think. A curious, open-ended question demonstrates strategic thinking. A confrontational or excessively vague one can do the opposite. Even the way you listen to their response—nodding, maintaining eye contact, following up thoughtfully—can shape their perception of you.

Thoughtful questions also allow you to set expectations and align visions. By asking about the team's current priorities, leadership style, or growth opportunities, you're showing that you're not just thinking about the job as it is today, but as it might evolve over time. This signals that you are forward-looking, someone who wants to grow with the organization rather than simply occupy a seat.

Equally important, asking the right questions can help you avoid future disappointment. Many people accept offers based on assumptions. They assume the culture will be supportive, the team will be collaborative, the leadership will be inspiring. But assumptions can lead to misalignment. Asking thoughtful questions lets you test those assumptions. It helps you understand whether the environment matches your expectations—and whether you'll be able to thrive in it.

This exchange of questions is also an opportunity to demonstrate confidence without arrogance. When your curiosity comes from a place of genuine interest rather than from trying to impress, it feels natural. You're not performing intelligence; you're expressing discernment. That distinction is subtle but powerful, and interviewers can feel it.

A candidate who approaches this part of the interview with care signals emotional maturity. They show they're not rushing to say yes to any offer—they want the right one. This also gives the interviewer a sense of partnership rather than hierarchy. Instead of being a passive recipient of an opportunity, you position yourself as someone who brings value, insight, and initiative to the table.

And finally, asking thoughtful questions shapes your own experience of the interview. Instead of walking away wondering whether the company is truly a good fit, you leave with a clearer picture. You walk away with insight, not just hope. That alone can make the difference between accepting an offer that energizes you and accepting one that drains you.

The power of thoughtful questions lies in their ability to shift the interview from a test into a dialogue. It turns an impersonal evaluation into a meaningful exchange between two professionals. It elevates your presence in the interviewer's mind, because you're no longer just another candidate—you're a potential collaborator, someone who understands the bigger picture.

This is why the last five minutes of an interview can be as influential as the first five. When you use that time to ask meaningful, well-considered questions, you leave behind a trace of depth. You don't need to be the loudest or the most charismatic candidate. Thoughtful curiosity speaks loudly on its own. It leaves a sense that you are someone who sees beyond the surface, someone who approaches their career with care.

When you step into that moment with intention, the interview stops being a one-way evaluation. It becomes a conversation about possibilities, about shared goals, about whether your future and theirs can align. And that is precisely the kind of moment that interviewers remember.

8.2 Turning Questions into Dialogue

When candidates reach the stage of asking their own questions, many treat it like the final scene of a performance: they deliver their lines, thank the interviewer, and wait to be dismissed. But this moment has far more potential than most people realize. It isn't just a chance to ask a few closing questions; it's an opportunity to transform the interaction from a one-sided evaluation into a genuine conversation. When you approach this stage with intention, you can create a sense of rapport that lingers long after the interview is over.

Turning questions into dialogue begins with shifting how you see this part of the interview. Instead of imagining it as a box to tick, see it as a chance to build connection. Up to this point, you've been responding to prompts designed to assess your fit. Now, you have the ability to guide the conversation in a way that reflects your curiosity, your values, and your ability to think strategically. This is not about delivering clever or rehearsed questions. It's about using your curiosity to open a space for meaningful exchange.

One of the most powerful ways to do this is to frame your questions not as detached queries but as invitations. The tone and structure of your question can either keep the conversation stiff and transactional or allow it to expand naturally. For example, a candidate who asks, "What are the company's biggest challenges right now?" will get an answer. But a candidate who follows up with, "That's interesting—how does the team approach those challenges in practice?" opens the door to a deeper discussion. The interviewer stops delivering answers and starts talking with you, not at you.

This subtle shift changes the energy in the room. Instead of feeling like an interviewer interrogating a candidate, it begins to feel like two professionals exploring possibilities together. That sense of ease doesn't just make the conversation more enjoyable; it makes you more memorable. Employers meet many candidates who deliver polished answers. They meet far fewer who create a real conversation.

A dialogue begins when you respond not only to the content of what they say but to the *human* behind it. If an interviewer shares something about their team's culture, challenges, or recent achievements, that's a doorway. A simple, genuine follow-up—"That sounds like a rewarding environment," or "That must have been a challenging project; how did your team handle that transition?"—invites them to share more. This exchange creates a small but powerful shift: you're no longer a stranger asking surface-level questions. You're someone who's engaged, listening, and genuinely interested.

This approach also helps reveal things that aren't on paper. Job descriptions are often polished and carefully worded, but the real story of a workplace is told in how people talk about it. When an interviewer answers your question in a natural conversation rather than a rehearsed soundbite, you get glimpses into the organization's culture, leadership style, and day-to-day realities.

This gives you richer information to decide whether the role is truly right for you.

Turning questions into dialogue also allows you to subtly demonstrate your own professional depth without forcing it. When you respond thoughtfully to their answers, when you share a relevant observation or experience, you show that you're already thinking like a colleague rather than just a candidate. This is especially powerful in more senior roles, but it applies at every level. The best interviews are not interrogations—they are conversations between people who might one day work together.

Another advantage of this conversational approach is that it makes you more relaxed. Many candidates feel intense pressure throughout the interview to deliver perfect answers. But when the interaction shifts into dialogue, it becomes more fluid. The interviewer relaxes too, and the tone becomes less formal, more authentic. This mutual easing often leaves a stronger final impression than a meticulously rehearsed closing line ever could.

It's also important to understand the timing of your follow-ups. Good dialogue isn't rushed. It's responsive. When the interviewer is speaking, give them space. Listen carefully. Don't interrupt to show how smart or engaged you are. Let them finish, then respond with a question or observation that builds naturally on what they've said. This shows respect and presence, which are qualities people remember.

The beauty of this approach is that it works even if you're not an extrovert. You don't need to dominate the conversation. You simply need to be present in it. A quiet but well-timed observation can have more weight than a long monologue. Dialogue isn't about performing; it's about connecting.

This dynamic also gives the interviewer a chance to talk about something they care about. Most hiring managers enjoy talking about their work when they feel someone is genuinely listening. When your questions spark that sense of genuine engagement, it leaves them feeling positive—not just about the company, but about you. They'll associate that feeling with your candidacy. And in competitive hiring decisions, impressions like this often tip the scale.

A strong dialogue can also offer insights into power dynamics and leadership style. If you ask about how decisions are made or how teams collaborate, the way the interviewer answers can reveal whether leadership is open or hierarchical, whether the culture is supportive or competitive. These aren't just nice-to-know details—they're clues about what your day-to-day reality would look like if you joined.

But for dialogue to be effective, it has to be genuine. Overly scripted or forced questions won't create the same impact. Interviewers can tell when someone is just trying to sound clever. Real curiosity is quieter. It shows up in the way you phrase your questions, the way you listen, the way you react to their answers. It doesn't have to be theatrical to be powerful.

This approach also helps level the playing field. When you create a meaningful exchange, you stop being just another candidate hoping for approval. You start to feel—and be perceived—as someone who is evaluating this opportunity with clarity and intention. That subtle shift in perception often leaves a lasting impression because it positions you as a peer, not a subordinate.

Turning questions into dialogue is not about controlling the conversation but about enriching it. It shows that you're not just thinking about how to get hired, but how to understand and align with the organization's values, challenges, and goals. It's a form of intellectual generosity: you're bringing your full self into the conversation, not just as an applicant, but as a thinking, curious, engaged human being.

This is the kind of interaction that sticks in an interviewer's mind. Long after the details of your résumé fade, they'll remember how the conversation felt—how you made the room feel a little more open, a little more real, a little more collaborative. And that memory often weighs more than people realize.

8.3 Reading Between the Lines

The answers you receive when you ask questions in an interview are just as important as the questions themselves—but not always in the obvious way. What people say is only part of the story. How they say it, what they emphasize, what they avoid, and the energy behind their words can tell you more about a workplace than any job description ever could. Reading between the lines is a skill that turns an ordinary interview into a genuine window into the company's culture.

This doesn't mean becoming suspicious or cynical. It means listening closely—not just to content, but to tone, pace, language, and emotional cues. When people speak about their work and their environment, their true feelings often slip through in subtle ways. If you're attentive, those details can give you valuable insights into whether the role and the organization are truly aligned with what you want.

For example, consider how someone answers a question about company culture. If their response is warm, vivid, and specific— if they speak about concrete examples of collaboration, growth, or shared purpose—that often signals authenticity. But if the answer is vague, flat, or overly rehearsed, it might suggest that the culture is less vibrant than they'd like you to believe. Vagueness isn't always a red flag, but it can be a sign that you should probe further.

The same principle applies to questions about leadership and decision-making. If an interviewer speaks clearly and confidently about how ideas are shared, how decisions are made, and how feedback is given, it signals transparency. If their answer is evasive, full of buzzwords but short on specifics, it may reveal a more rigid or unclear structure. How they talk about power often reflects how power is actually experienced within the organization.

Another powerful clue comes from body language. When people talk about aspects of their work they're proud of, their energy tends to shift—they sit up straighter, their tone becomes more animated, their eyes brighten. When they discuss something more sensitive, their posture may tighten, their answers shorten, their voice flattens. These are not foolproof signals, but they're meaningful when combined with context.

Reading between the lines also means paying attention to what *isn't* said. Sometimes what's omitted reveals as much as what's shared. If you ask about career development and get a vague answer, it may indicate a lack of structured growth opportunities. If you ask about how the company supports employees during challenges and the response quickly changes subject, it may be worth exploring further.

This kind of listening requires presence. If you're too focused on delivering your next question perfectly, you'll miss the nuances in their response. But if you listen with genuine curiosity, you'll start to pick up on layers beneath the surface.

A common mistake candidates make is taking everything said in an interview at face value. Most companies want to present themselves in the best possible light, just as candidates do. That's natural. But by listening attentively, you can distinguish between polished narratives and authentic reflections. An interviewer who can acknowledge challenges honestly and talk about how the company addresses them is often a more reliable source of truth than one who insists everything is perfect.

Reading between the lines isn't about being skeptical; it's about being discerning. It's about noticing whether their words align with their tone and demeanor. When someone's words and energy are aligned, it usually means they're telling the truth. When they're out of sync, it's worth paying closer attention.

It's also valuable to observe how people talk about their colleagues. Do they speak with warmth and respect, or in detached, corporate language? How someone talks about their team can reveal a lot about the actual human dynamics behind the formal structure.

Similarly, when you ask about work-life balance, listen carefully not just to the answer but to the way it's delivered. If they seem hesitant, overemphasize perks, or avoid giving specifics, it might indicate a more demanding environment than they're willing to state outright. On the other hand, if they speak clearly about boundaries, flexibility, and respect for personal time, it can be a sign of a healthier culture.

This ability to read between the lines can protect you from accepting a role that isn't truly what it seems. Many candidates fall in love with the idea of a job based on surface impressions, only to discover after joining that the culture, expectations, or leadership don't align with their values. Careful listening during the interview can help you spot misalignments before they become lived frustrations.

But beyond protecting yourself, this skill also enhances how you show up in the interview. When you engage deeply with the interviewer's answers, when you respond thoughtfully to what they actually mean, you elevate the conversation. It shows that you're not just asking questions to perform interest. You're paying attention. You're discerning.

This creates a quiet but powerful impression. Employers are not just looking for people who can do the work. They're looking for people who understand nuance, who can navigate complexity, who listen deeply. When you demonstrate this capacity, you stand out—not because you said something flashy, but because you brought depth to the conversation.

Reading between the lines also builds your confidence in making decisions. It shifts your mindset from "I hope they pick me" to "I'm evaluating whether this is right for me." That's an entirely different energy, one that interviewers can sense. It positions you as a peer, not as someone passively waiting for approval.

Over time, this skill becomes second nature. You stop clinging to rehearsed scripts and start inhabiting the conversation fully. You notice more. You think more clearly. You ask better follow-ups. And you make choices that reflect not just opportunity, but alignment.

In the end, asking good questions is only half the equation. Listening to the answers—truly listening, beyond the surface—is what transforms a standard interview into a moment of clarity. It's what allows you to leave the room not just hoping for the best, but knowing more deeply whether this is a place where you can belong, contribute, and thrive.

That clarity is a quiet kind of power. It isn't loud or dramatic. But it stays with you long after the interview ends, guiding your decisions with confidence and calm. And employers, whether consciously or not, respect the kind of candidate who brings that kind of presence into the room.

Chapter 9: Navigating Offers and Negotiations with Confidence

9.1 Understanding Your Value Before the Offer

The period between a successful interview and receiving an offer can feel like standing at the threshold of a new life. For many candidates, it's a mix of excitement and anxiety. After weeks or even months of searching, interviewing, and proving themselves, they finally sense the possibility of an offer. And yet, this is also the stage where many people give away their power without even realizing it. They see the offer as something to be accepted or rejected, rather than a conversation to be navigated with clarity, confidence, and self-respect.

Understanding your value *before* the offer lands is one of the most decisive factors in shaping your professional future. If you walk into this stage unprepared, you risk accepting less than you deserve, agreeing to terms that don't reflect your worth, or saying yes to a situation that doesn't align with your goals. But when you know your value—when you've clarified not just what you want but why—you enter the negotiation as a participant, not a passive recipient.

Many people feel uncomfortable with negotiation. They see it as confrontational, something only people with aggressive personalities or endless leverage can do well. This is a misconception. Negotiation is not a battle; it's a structured conversation about aligning interests. When done with the right mindset, it's an act of mutual respect, not aggression. Employers expect it. In many cases, they even respect candidates more when they negotiate thoughtfully, because it signals self-awareness and professionalism.

But successful negotiation begins well before the offer arrives. It starts with preparation—deep, honest preparation about what you bring to the table and what matters to you. Without this inner work, even the best opportunities can lead to disappointment.

The first step is to shift your mindset around value. Value is not just about how many years of experience you have, your job title, or the technical skills on your résumé. It's about the combination of your abilities, your perspective, your capacity to solve problems, and your potential to make a meaningful impact. Employers don't make offers out of charity. They make offers because they believe you can bring something of real worth to their team.

To understand your value clearly, you need to examine both your hard and soft contributions. The hard side is easier to articulate: skills, expertise, certifications, achievements, quantifiable results. These give employers tangible reasons to invest in you. But the soft side—your ability to lead, collaborate, communicate, think critically, adapt—is equally, if not more, influential. Many candidates overlook this dimension because it's harder to measure. But in many roles, it's what sets top performers apart.

Understanding your value also involves seeing yourself in context. It's not about inflating your worth or minimizing it. It's about understanding where your strengths fit into the organization's needs. If you've done your research during the interview process, you should already have a sense of what problems the company is trying to solve, what kind of culture it fosters, and what kind of person they need. Your value is clearest when you can see how your abilities align with those needs.

This is why reflecting on your past accomplishments is so crucial. Not in a vague, self-congratulatory way, but with specificity. What problems have you solved? What impact did your work have on your previous teams, clients, or organizations? How did you create change or improve something? Being able to speak about these moments with clarity and confidence gives you a solid foundation for negotiating from strength.

But knowing your value isn't just about what you can offer. It's also about understanding what you need to thrive. Too many candidates accept offers that look good on paper but ignore crucial factors like work-life balance, growth opportunities, team dynamics, or alignment with their personal values. Over time, those overlooked factors can lead to dissatisfaction, burnout, or the quiet sense of having settled.

This is why before entering any negotiation, it's essential to clarify your priorities. What are your non-negotiables? What matters deeply to you in a role? It could be salary, but it might also be autonomy, creative freedom, schedule flexibility, meaningful work, or opportunities to grow. Knowing this ahead of time prevents you from making emotional decisions in the heat of the moment. It also gives your negotiation more focus.

It's equally important to research the market. Confidence is not built in a vacuum. It comes from being informed. Understanding what professionals with your skills and experience are paid in your region or industry gives you a realistic sense of your worth. It prevents you from underselling yourself out of insecurity or overpricing yourself out of alignment. Market knowledge is a shield against both self-doubt and blind guesswork.

But value isn't only about numbers. Many negotiations go beyond base salary. Companies often have room to be flexible in other areas: signing bonuses, stock options, professional development opportunities, additional leave, flexible working arrangements. Knowing what matters most to you allows you to navigate these elements intelligently rather than treating the offer as a fixed, take-it-or-leave-it scenario.

Understanding your value before the offer also means being ready to say no if necessary. This doesn't mean rejecting offers recklessly. It means having a clear sense of your boundaries and self-respect. Saying no to something that doesn't align with your needs can be more powerful than saying yes to something that diminishes you. It can open the door to better opportunities that truly match your value.

However, this kind of confidence doesn't come from arrogance. It comes from quiet preparation. It comes from being honest with yourself about your worth, your goals, and your priorities. Candidates who have done this inner work radiate a different kind of energy when offers come in. They don't rush to accept out of fear. They take a breath, evaluate carefully, and engage in a dialogue.

Understanding your value also changes the way you communicate during the final stages of the interview process. When you know your worth, your language naturally becomes more assertive—not in a harsh or entitled way, but in a way that conveys clarity and self-assurance. Instead of saying, "I'll take whatever you offer," you might say, "I'm looking for a role that reflects both my skills and the impact I can bring. Here's where I see my range based on market research and my experience." This kind of language shifts the conversation from a one-sided offer to a shared negotiation.

Another key part of understanding your value is acknowledging what makes you unique. Many candidates undervalue themselves because they compare their skills to others or assume that their contributions are replaceable. But your specific combination of experience, perspective, and strengths is not interchangeable.

Even in competitive markets, employers choose individuals because of how they fit, not just because of their skill set.

And while numbers and benefits are important, value goes deeper than compensation. It's about understanding the worth of your time, your energy, and your potential. An offer that looks financially generous but comes at the cost of your well-being or growth is not a good offer. A role that aligns with your purpose, supports your development, and values your contribution can be worth more in the long run, even if the numbers are modest at first.

Another common trap candidates fall into is rushing the process out of fear of losing the offer. But an employer who truly values you won't pull an offer simply because you want time to consider it thoughtfully. Taking time to assess isn't a sign of weakness—it's a sign of discernment. When you pause, you send a signal that you're not desperate. You're careful, strategic, and aware of your value.

This preparation also gives you more leverage. Negotiation isn't about demanding. It's about aligning value. When you can articulate clearly why you're worth what you're asking for—not just because you want it, but because your contribution justifies it—you give employers a reason to meet you where you are.

The final, perhaps most important, element of understanding your value before the offer is remembering that the offer is not a gift. It's a professional agreement. Employers are not doing you a favor by hiring you; they're making a decision that benefits both sides. When you hold that truth close, you stop shrinking yourself in the process. You start standing on equal ground.

This doesn't make negotiations easy, but it makes them honest. It allows you to approach the conversation with steadiness rather than fear. And that steadiness is what employers remember. A candidate who knows their worth isn't reckless or arrogant. They are clear, composed, and respectful—both of themselves and of the organization.

Understanding your value before the offer is, at its core, about agency. It's about reclaiming your power in a process where many people unconsciously give it away. When you know what you bring, what you need, and what you stand for, you walk into the negotiation not as someone waiting for approval, but as someone ready to build a partnership. That's the kind of energy that doesn't just get offers. It gets the *right* offers. And more importantly, it lays the foundation for a career built on mutual respect, not silent compromise.

9.2 Negotiating Without Fear

For many people, the word "negotiation" triggers a knot in the stomach. It carries connotations of tension, conflict, or even personal risk. Candidates worry about sounding ungrateful, losing the offer, or coming across as difficult. But at its essence, negotiation is neither a battle nor a test of charm. It is a structured conversation between two parties with overlapping interests, both trying to create an agreement that makes sense for each of them. Understanding this shifts the energy entirely. It stops feeling like a confrontation and begins to feel like a collaboration.

The biggest obstacle most people face when negotiating is fear—fear of asking for more, fear of being judged, fear of not seeming "worth it." This fear often stems from deeply ingrained cultural and personal beliefs: that asking for more is impolite, that the first offer must be accepted, or that you should be grateful just to be chosen. But the truth is that negotiation is not a sign of greed or entitlement; it is a sign of self-respect. Employers expect negotiation. In fact, for many hiring managers, a candidate who doesn't negotiate at all may come across as either unaware of their market value or lacking confidence.

Overcoming fear begins with reframing the purpose of negotiation. It's not about "winning" or "taking" something from the other side. It's about ensuring that the agreement reflects reality—your skills, your contributions, your needs, and their expectations. When you see it this way, negotiation becomes less of a performance and more of an honest conversation about alignment. You're not begging for more; you're defining what makes sense.

Another source of fear comes from the belief that the offer is fragile, that pushing back will make it disappear. While there are exceptions, in most professional environments this is not true. If an employer has reached the point of making you an offer, they've invested time, energy, and resources into the process. They've decided they want you. Reasonable, respectful negotiation doesn't undo that—it often strengthens their respect for you. It shows you value your work and can advocate for yourself, which are often qualities they value in their team members as well.

The way you negotiate matters as much as what you negotiate for. Many people approach this conversation with either too much deference or too much aggression. The sweet spot is calm confidence. This means being clear about what matters to you, expressing it without apology, and framing the discussion as a shared effort to find common ground. You're not fighting against the employer; you're working *with* them to reach an agreement that benefits both sides.

An effective negotiation often starts with gratitude and clarity. Expressing appreciation for the offer and excitement for the opportunity creates a collaborative tone. From there, you can state your position clearly: what elements of the offer you'd like to discuss, why they matter, and how they align with your value. For example, instead of simply saying "I want more," you can articulate the reasoning behind your request—your skills, your experience, your market research, your responsibilities. This turns a vague demand into a clear, reasoned conversation.

It's also important to understand that negotiation doesn't always have to be about salary alone. In fact, some of the most meaningful improvements to an offer come from other areas: flexibility in schedule, opportunities for professional development, stock options, bonuses, relocation support, or additional time off. By broadening your perspective, you give both yourself and the employer more room to find a mutually satisfying solution. This is particularly helpful if salary bands are fixed and there's limited flexibility on base pay.

Confidence in negotiation does not mean arrogance. It means knowing your worth and communicating it with respect. Fear often makes people either retreat completely or overcompensate by being overly forceful. But real confidence has a quiet steadiness to it. You can say, "Based on my skills and what I've seen in the market, I was hoping for something closer to X" without needing to inflate your language or diminish yourself. You can pause, let your words land, and allow the conversation to unfold.

One of the biggest mistakes people make is rushing to fill the silence after making their request. Silence can feel uncomfortable, especially when money or terms are involved. But silence is not your enemy. Often, the other party needs a moment to think, to review internally, or to respond thoughtfully. If you rush in to soften your statement or backtrack, you undermine your own position. Trust the pause. Let your words breathe.

Another essential part of negotiating without fear is emotional neutrality. Negotiation can stir up personal insecurities, especially if your sense of worth is tangled up with the offer amount. But remember, this is not a personal judgment of your worth as a person. It's a conversation about compensation for a role. When you separate your self-worth from the negotiation, you can approach it more calmly and clearly.

It's also worth noting that negotiation can build respect. Many candidates assume employers dislike negotiation. But seasoned managers often respect candidates who advocate for themselves intelligently. It signals that you're thoughtful, aware of your value, and capable of handling complex conversations—qualities that are often highly desirable in an employee.

The key is to be prepared. Confidence comes from clarity, and clarity comes from preparation. If you've done your research, understood your value, and know what matters to you, your negotiation will feel less like improvisation and more like dialogue. You won't need to bluff or posture, because your position will rest on solid ground.

It's equally important to know what flexibility you have. Not every request will be met exactly as stated. But negotiation isn't about ultimatums; it's about creating options. Sometimes, employers may not meet your salary request but can offer other forms of compensation or benefits that make the overall package more appealing. When you approach the conversation with openness rather than fear, you give both sides room to collaborate.

Finally, a crucial aspect of negotiating without fear is giving yourself permission to walk away if necessary. Not in a combative way, but in a way that reflects self-respect. If an offer doesn't meet your core needs and there's no room for movement, walking away isn't failure—it's clarity. Knowing you have the power to decline frees you from desperation and lets you negotiate from a position of dignity rather than fear.

Negotiation is not a battlefield. It's a bridge. And the strength of that bridge depends on how you approach it. When you step into the conversation with preparation, respect, and quiet confidence, the fear that once loomed large begins to fade. In its place comes a steadier truth: that your voice matters, and that asking for what you need is not a risk—it's a right.

9.3 Evaluating the Full Offer Beyond Salary

When most people think about a job offer, their focus narrows to a single figure: the salary. It's understandable. Salary is tangible, measurable, and often the clearest indicator of how an employer values your work. But a job offer is much more than a number. It's a complex equation that includes not only your pay but also your time, your energy, your well-being, your opportunities for growth, and your overall quality of life. Evaluating the full offer with a wide lens can mean the difference between a job that simply pays and one that truly supports your long-term goals.

Many candidates make the mistake of saying yes to the highest number they see, only to discover months later that the role demands unsustainable hours, offers no meaningful development opportunities, or places them in a culture that drains rather than fuels them. Others fixate on a salary that's slightly below their expectations and overlook a benefits package that, taken as a whole, might actually create a better quality of life. Looking at the complete picture requires slowing down and thinking holistically about what truly matters to you.

The first dimension to consider beyond salary is time. Time is the invisible currency that shapes your daily reality. A job with a slightly lower salary but genuine respect for work-life balance can end up being worth far more to your well-being than a higher-paying position that demands constant overtime or emotional exhaustion. Ask yourself: how many hours will this role truly require? What expectations exist around availability, weekends, or after-hours communication? A generous paycheck can lose its luster quickly if it comes at the cost of your health, your relationships, or your sense of freedom.

Next, consider benefits and perks, not in a superficial way, but in terms of their real impact on your life. Health insurance, retirement contributions, wellness programs, professional development allowances, childcare support, transportation benefits—these are all forms of compensation, even if they don't appear in the headline number. A strong benefits package can significantly increase your total compensation and reduce your personal expenses in meaningful ways.

Flexibility is another critical factor. The world of work has shifted dramatically, and for many professionals, the ability to work remotely or have flexible hours is as valuable as money, if not more. If an employer offers flexible scheduling, remote work options, or a hybrid structure that gives you greater autonomy over your time, that can fundamentally change how sustainable the role feels.

Career growth potential is perhaps one of the most underestimated parts of an offer. A job that pays slightly less today but offers real opportunities for advancement, learning, and skill-building can become far more valuable over time. When evaluating an offer, ask yourself not only what the job will give you now but also where it can take you in one, three, or five years. Does the company invest in employee development? Are there clear paths to grow, or is it a role with little room to evolve?

Another often-overlooked factor is company culture. No amount of money compensates for a toxic or misaligned work environment. If your interviews have given you a sense of how the team interacts, how leadership communicates, and what values the organization lives by, that information is invaluable. A respectful, supportive culture can make your work meaningful and sustainable. A rigid or disrespectful one can make even the best salary feel like a trap.

You should also consider the stability of the company or organization. A generous offer from a company on shaky financial ground might be less appealing than a slightly lower offer from an organization with a strong track record of growth and security. Stability provides peace of mind, and peace of mind is its own form of compensation.

Geography and commuting should also be factored in. A high salary can be undermined by long commutes, relocation costs, or a significantly higher cost of living in a new city. Sometimes, a slightly lower salary closer to home or in a more affordable location can lead to a higher quality of life overall.

Additionally, think about how this role aligns with your personal values and goals. Does it support the kind of life you want to build, or does it pull you away from it? This alignment often reveals itself in subtle ways—through how the company talks about its mission, how it treats its employees, and how your role contributes to something larger. When your work aligns with your deeper values, it tends to feel less like a transaction and more like a meaningful endeavor.

Another essential element to evaluate is autonomy. How much decision-making power will you have in this role? Will you have room to bring your ideas forward, or will you be expected to simply execute tasks? For many people, a sense of agency is worth more than incremental salary increases. Having the freedom to shape your workday, contribute creatively, and grow your responsibilities over time can make your professional life richer and more fulfilling.

Workplace structure and leadership style are also powerful influences. A supportive, transparent leadership team can make a challenging role rewarding, while poor leadership can make even a well-compensated position unbearable. Pay attention to how leadership was described during your interviews, how they communicate, and how they respond to questions. Those cues often reveal more than formal job descriptions ever could.

Another layer to consider is how the offer aligns with your personal circumstances outside of work. If you have family responsibilities, health considerations, or personal projects, the flexibility and understanding of your employer can be as critical as the paycheck. An employer who supports work-life integration and respects boundaries can dramatically improve your overall well-being.

Evaluating the full offer means thinking like a strategist rather than just a job seeker. It's not about chasing the highest immediate number but about choosing the right foundation for the next chapter of your life. A strong offer is one that aligns with your financial goals, your personal values, and your long-term vision. It should make sense both on paper and in practice.

Finally, evaluating an offer holistically gives you confidence when negotiating. When you understand the full landscape, you can approach discussions not from a place of blind insistence on a single number but from an informed perspective that considers multiple variables. That flexibility makes negotiations smoother, more respectful, and more likely to result in a mutually satisfying agreement.

The 8-Week Plan to Get a New Job

A job offer is not just a paycheck. It is an agreement that shapes your daily reality, your growth trajectory, and your sense of purpose. When you evaluate the full offer with clarity and intention, you step into your next chapter not just as someone who has landed a role, but as someone who has chosen it deliberately. And that choice—rooted in awareness and self-respect—can change the entire arc of your professional journey.

Conclusion: Stepping Into the Next Chapter with Confidence

The journey of finding and securing a meaningful job is rarely straightforward. It's not just about crafting a polished résumé, performing well in interviews, or negotiating a fair offer. It's a deeply human process—one that requires clarity, self-awareness, and the courage to trust your own value. By the time you reach the end of such a journey, you're not the same person who began it. Something within you has shifted. You've sharpened your understanding of what matters, learned to communicate your worth more clearly, and discovered that success in the professional world is not simply a matter of luck or timing, but of preparation, intention, and presence.

Throughout this process, there has been a recurring theme: agency. Too often, people approach the job search as passive participants. They apply, wait, hope, and accept. They treat opportunities as something handed to them rather than something they can shape. But when you step into your search with strategy, when you learn to present your story with authenticity and clarity, when you ask thoughtful questions, and when you negotiate with respect and confidence, you transform that passivity into power. You become a co-architect of your path, not a spectator in someone else's decision.

At the heart of this transformation lies the understanding that work is not just about a paycheck. It's about meaning, growth, and alignment. A job is a space where your time, energy, and talent intersect with an organization's mission, culture, and needs. When those elements align, something far greater than employment takes shape. You step into a role that allows you to contribute, to evolve, to build a life that reflects who you are and where you want to go.

This is why the early steps of the journey—defining your goals, clarifying your value, identifying what truly matters to you—are not simply administrative tasks. They are acts of self-respect. They set the foundation for everything that follows. If you begin your job search anchored in a clear sense of self, every decision along the way becomes less clouded by doubt. You stop chasing opportunities that don't fit. You stop accepting less than what you deserve. You start moving with purpose.

The interview, too, is no longer something to fear but an opportunity to connect. When you enter that room—or log into that call—with preparation, grounded confidence, and curiosity, you stop seeing the interviewer as an obstacle. You see them as a human being on the other side of the table, someone also navigating the complexities of work and decision-making. This shift changes everything. Instead of performing, you engage. Instead of trying to prove your worth frantically, you let it speak quietly through clarity, presence, and thoughtful dialogue.

A crucial part of this journey is embracing discomfort. Uncertainty is built into every transition. The moments before a big interview, the silence after sending out an application, the delicate dance of negotiation—these are not signs that something is wrong. They are signs that you are stretching, growing, and stepping into territory where your future is being shaped. Confidence doesn't mean eliminating discomfort. It means learning to walk with it, letting it sharpen rather than paralyze you.

Negotiation, in particular, is a powerful moment of truth. It's where many people, without even realizing it, hand their power away. But when you enter this stage with a clear understanding of your worth—not inflated, not diminished, but real—you begin to see negotiation for what it is: a conversation, not a fight. You realize that asking for what you deserve isn't selfish; it's responsible. It sets the tone for your relationship with the organization, not as someone desperate to be accepted, but as someone who respects both themselves and the partnership being built.

Yet the journey doesn't end when you sign the offer letter. That moment, while significant, is just the doorway to something larger. How you step through that doorway matters just as much as how you arrived at it. The first ninety days of a new role are a time when impressions are formed, trust is built, and your presence begins to take root. This is not a time to strive for perfection, but for intentionality. Showing up consistently, listening deeply, observing carefully, and contributing meaningfully will do more to shape your path than trying to dazzle anyone with theatrical brilliance.

It's in those early days that the invisible threads of trust and connection begin to weave. You learn who your allies are, who holds quiet influence, how the culture truly works beneath the surface of official messaging. You learn when to speak and when to listen, when to step forward and when to observe. If you navigate this phase with awareness rather than haste, you give yourself the gift of integration rather than mere arrival.

Another key truth that emerges along this path is that your career is not a single decision, but an ongoing series of choices. Some will be bold leaps, others small adjustments. Some will lead to immediate clarity, others will only make sense in hindsight. But each choice becomes more intentional when it's guided by self-awareness rather than fear. A job offer is never the end; it is one chapter in a long and evolving story. How you begin that chapter sets the tone for the next.

One of the most empowering realizations for any professional is that confidence is not something you're given. It's something you build through repeated acts of showing up for yourself. It grows in the moments when you speak clearly about your skills. It grows when you hold your ground during negotiation. It grows when you walk into a new environment with both humility and quiet strength. It's not loud or boastful; it's steady and enduring.

The process of finding and starting a new job is also an act of resilience. There will be setbacks. You may face rejections that sting. You may have interviews that don't go as planned. You may encounter silence that feels personal but isn't. These moments do not diminish your value. They are simply part of the terrain. Every rejection clears the way for an opportunity better aligned with who you are. Every awkward moment teaches you something about how to show up more fully next time.

And perhaps most importantly, this journey teaches you to stop seeking external validation as your only measure of worth. Your value does not depend on whether a single company says yes. It's rooted in your skills, your integrity, your perspective, and your capacity to contribute meaningfully. A job offer doesn't define you. How you navigate the journey toward it does.

It's also worth remembering that careers are rarely linear. You may pivot, shift industries, move across borders, or reinvent your path entirely. The ability to do so with clarity and confidence comes from mastering the underlying skills this process teaches: knowing your worth, communicating it with authenticity, asking the right questions, negotiating wisely, and integrating into new spaces with grace. These are not just job-hunting skills—they are life skills.

As you move forward, carry with you the knowledge that every interaction matters. A thoughtful question can reveal a truth you wouldn't have otherwise seen. A well-placed pause can turn an uncertain moment into one of quiet strength. A carefully negotiated offer can change the trajectory of your career. A steady, observant first ninety days can lay the groundwork for years of meaningful growth.

But above all, remember that this journey is about alignment. It's about finding work that doesn't just fill your days, but expands your sense of purpose. It's about stepping into spaces where your contribution matters, where your growth is nurtured, and where you can build something that reflects who you are becoming.

No one can hand you that alignment. It's something you cultivate with patience and persistence, with reflection and courage. It's something you claim when you decide that your career will be shaped not by fear or by luck, but by your deliberate, thoughtful actions.

If there's one lasting truth to hold on to, it's this: You have more power than you think. The way you prepare, the way you communicate, the way you choose and negotiate, the way you begin—these are not small things. They are the building blocks of a career defined not just by survival, but by purpose.

Stepping into a new chapter doesn't require perfection. It requires clarity, courage, and a willingness to trust the foundation you've built for yourself. It requires remembering that you bring something unique to the table—not just a set of skills, but a perspective, a story, a way of showing up that no one else can replicate.

So as you move forward, let your actions be guided not by the fear of being chosen, but by the certainty that you are also choosing. Let your conversations be driven not by anxiety, but by curiosity. Let your first days in a new role reflect not desperation to prove yourself, but a steady intention to grow, connect, and contribute.

This is your career. It is your time, your energy, your story. Treat it with the seriousness it deserves, and the world begins to respond differently to you. Not because it suddenly becomes easy, but because you walk through it differently—no longer as someone waiting to be seen, but as someone who already knows their worth.

That is the quiet strength at the heart of every successful transition. And it's a strength that, once claimed, will carry you not just through one job, but through a lifetime of purposeful, meaningful work.

www.ingramcontent.com/pod-product-compliance
Lightning Source LLC
Chambersburg PA
CBHW051945160426
43198CB00013B/2308